THE CHALK DUST
COLLECTION

Thoughts and Reflections on Teaching in Colleges and Universities

Linc. Fisch

 NEW FORUMS PRESS INC.
Stillwater, Oklahoma

The chapters listed below have been reprinted with special permission of the original publisher.

Chapters 1, 12, and 34 originally appeared in *To Improve the Academy*, the annual sourcebook published by The Professional and Organizational Development Network in Higher Education.

Chapters 2, 3, 5, 6, 7, 9, 10, 11, 13, 14, 15, 16, 17, 18, 19, 21, 22, 23, 25, 27, 28, 29, 30, 32, and 33 originally appeared in *The Journal of Staff, Program, & Organization Development*.

Chapters 4 and 31 originally appeared in *Connexions*, published by the International Society for Exploring Teaching Alternatives.

Chapter 8 originally appeared in *Innovation Abstracts*, published by the National Institute for Staff and Organizational Development.

Chapter 20 originally appeared in *College Teaching*.

Chapter 35 originally appeared in *Teaching Excellence*, published by The POD Network.

Dedication

To E.E.W.

Good colleague,
critic, and friend
for many years.

Policy on reproducing chapters from this collection

Chapters contained herein are copyrighted but may be reproduced on a limited basis, subject to the following conditions:

- The use of such copies must be for non-profit educational purposes, such as reprinting in campus newsletters or distributing in classes and workshops.

- A request must be submitted to New Forums Press stating the intended use, number of copies, and medium of distribution. Ordinarily, permission for one-time use will be granted for up to three requests from any one agency or person.

- If duplication is done through reprocessing of text (rather than direct photocopying) a final copy before printing must be submitted for review and approval by New Forums Press.

- Upon request, the publisher will provide a computer disk of a chapter at a nominal charge for the disk, processing, and shipping.

- Chapters must be reproduced in their entirety unless special permission for changes in text or title are cleared with the author.

- Copies must carry a complete bibliographical attribution, including title of both collection and chapter, author, publisher, date, and the statement "Reprinted with special permission of the author and publisher."

- Subsequent to printing, two copies of the publication containing the chapter must be sent to the publisher.

- Quotations and excerpts not exceeding 150 words may be printed without following the above policy as long as appropriate attribution to the source is made.

All questions concerning this duplication policy should be directed to New Forums Press, Inc., P.O. Box 876, Stillwater, OK 74076 (Phone 405-372-6158; fax 405-377-2237; email address newforums@aol.com)

Contents

Foreword

Linc. Fisch's writings are, I believe, the best combination of wit and wisdom in all of higher education. In these short essays he spans a broad range of topics: from the first day of class to cross-country trucking, from coaching to teaching calculus, from seven great truths of teaching to Mozart—and a multitude more of interest and value. All of the essays are entertaining and engaging, but the important thing is that they also provoke thought, provide new insights, and offer practical advice to all of us in college teaching—young or old, novice or emeritus, scientist or humanist.

When I received the manuscript, I thought that I would simply skim a few of the articles, since I had read many of them before. Yet once I started, I kept on with continuous enjoyment and thoughts of "That's right!"

But this is not a book to be read straight through. Most pieces are two to four pages long and stand by themselves. Each deals succinctly with a particular concept or thought relevant to teaching—often from an unusual perspective. Each is worth reflecting upon. And all contain ideas that can be implemented in the classroom.

Any who have responsibility for improving teaching—deans, chairs, supervisors of teaching assistants, and, indeed, every faculty member—will find a gold mine here. Campus editors will discover a rich lode of material that may be extracted and reprinted in newsletters. The length and style of the essays are such that even faculty members who rarely are willing to take time for anything about higher education and teaching might actually read one or more of them.

Start browsing. You'll find both stimulation and fun.

Wilbert J. McKeachie

To the Reader

This book is a collection of short articles on college teaching that I've written during the past dozen years. Most of them have been published in professional journals, many in a column called "Chalk Dust" in *The Journal of Staff, Program, & Organization Development* .

The articles reflect my conviction that what can be read quickly is more likely to be read. In addition, I've discovered that articles are more likely to be remembered and applied when the perspective of the writer is fresh or novel. These two principles largely inform my writing.

I have not tried to be comprehensive in dealing with college teaching. The topics have grown out of my experiences and my reflection thereon. Another of my convictions is that there is meaning to be found in almost any experience or event if one is tuned in to examining it carefully enough. Thus, the settings for these pieces vary widely—stadium, kitchen, garden, mountains, bar, dental office (to identify just a few).

The articles are in no special strategic order, and they may be read serially or selectively. I've included short descriptive notes with the titles to assist readers who wish to do the latter.

Some of the articles present specific information and may even reach conclusions. Others are open-ended, allowing readers to come to their own decisions about the subject. I intend for all of them to stimulate thought and action about teaching.

In order to facilitate that, space follows each article so that the reader may jot down notes, reactions, and responses. I particularly hope that this will encourage readers to identify one or more actions that they will undertake as a result of reading the article. In this regard, being specific about the action—in what course and when it will take place—will help insure that intent will not get lost among the everyday rush and reality of academic life, things that legitimately require our attention but in the long run may be less important than teaching well.

I've had many suggestions concerning use of these articles for readings in courses on college teaching, as discussion pieces for faculty luncheons and seminars, and for distribution to faculty members or teaching assistants. In order to accommodate such use, the articles have been set to facilitate photocopying, and I've negotiated a rather liberal reprint procedure with my very cooperative publisher [see statement on page iv].

It's probably evident that I've enjoyed writing these pieces. I hope you'll enjoy reading them. I've found the writing of them to be beneficial in my work, and I hope that similarly you will find stimulus, meaning, and value in the reading—and in the actions you take as a result thereof.

Linc. Fisch
Lexington, Kentucky
April 1, 1996

Coaching Mathematics and Other Academic Sports

My colleagues in music, drama, and athletics did not just teach—they coached. *I learned many useful concepts about my instructional role from them.*

It was one of those gorgeous autumn afternoons: a deep October blue sky contrasted with the brilliant golds and crimsons of the trees, the dazzle of the sun moderated the crispness in the air, and the spirit of the Homecoming crowd brought the stadium to vibrant life. It was a perfect day for football—and hardly the time or the place to be meditating about teaching. But that's where I first began to wonder—to wonder why the football coach seemed to have so much more success with his team than I had with my mathematics class. A strange thought it was.

After the game, I decided to ask the coach the secret of his success. And then I talked with other colleagues in music and drama. It was an odd collection of consultants, but they had one thing in common: they all coached students. They did not just teach, they *coached.* And they all seemed more successful than I, who merely "taught" students. Why?

For one thing, these coaches worked a lot with students on an individual basis. To be sure, they also dealt with students in groups—a team, a choir, a cast—just as I dealt with students in a class. But the crux of their work was individual coaching, something I found that I rarely did. And when I did work with students individually, it was more or less a miniature version of what I did in the classroom every day: explain theory, work problems, ask a few questions.

One big difference was that I rarely asked my students to perform, other than on infrequent hour tests. The coaches were always asking their charges to perform *under observation*—to run plays, to sing arias, to act out roles in rehearsals prior to their big tests. And another big difference was how the coaches dealt with student performance. They carefully reinforced correct performance—one step at a time. They pointed out wrong stances, flat pitches, inappropriate inflections. Then they had students practice repeatedly until one behavior was correct before going on to another.

What did *I* do? I *showed* students how to work problems, whole problems, with several steps carefully ordered in logical sequence. If the students nodded, I assumed that they understood and I went on to other problems. Imagine a football coach himself throwing passes and running plays with precision throughout practices while his players watched him—and then leaving them on their own and expecting them to do the same things just as well on the day of the game!

I quickly realized that I might not have time to coach all my students individually all the time. Some talented ones seemed to do pretty well without frequent attention, so I focused my efforts on those who were barely "making the team"—my team—academically. I invited them—no, that's not the word—I *urged* them, and even required some to come to my office for one-on-one coaching sessions. Sometimes I opened these with a brief example to illustrate a concept. More often, I posed a problem and had the student work it on my office blackboard. I was careful to provide reinforcement for correct and proper procedures. I provided guidance only as necessary, and I pointed out inappropriate behaviors—one at a time. Then I had the student correct that behavior and practice on similar problems until I felt sure that the technique in question was mastered. I discovered that even the better students sometimes needed to correct little mistakes of which they had never been aware. In addition, I tried to ask questions that allowed the student to organize and summarize, rather than do these things myself.

It was challenging work and it was harder work than I had been doing, but it seemed to pay off in terms of learning. Grades on tests improved and the response from students was quite favorable. I realized that I was putting into practice some principles that I always knew were valid: positive reinforcement and immediate knowledge of results. Somehow these had gotten lost in the shuffle of dividing courses into weeks and days and in the process of covering material "efficiently."

There was an interesting carryover into my daily classroom activities. I found myself asking more questions in class and asking questions more effectively. I was consciously mixing coaching strategies with my customary presentation strategies. I was viewing students more as individuals than collectively as a class. I also began to reduce the time between examinations and to incorporate more short quizzes. (In one course I eventually replaced all the hour exams with a pattern of frequent quizzes.) I found it more effective to respond to incorrect problems one at a time, rather than to dump as many as a dozen corrections on a student at once, as had sometimes been the case previously when I graded an hour exam. (The coach never waited until half-time to give his quarterback a truckload of criticisms and suggestions!) And I found myself making a point to write positive comments more often on examinations before I returned them to students.

Yet, I wasn't quite satisfied. I went back to the football field for more pointers and more consultation. I noticed some other things that happened there. Players practiced with each other—blocking, tackling, chucking, and all those special behaviors that have begun to make football a complicated (if not fine) art and science these days. Often, they corrected each other without any help from the coach. I decided to have my students sometimes come to coaching sessions in pairs to work with each other, and I encouraged them to continue to do so on their own. Some of them, having experienced the value of working together, did so and reported favorably. In one class, collaboration evolved into a system for students to prepare and post solutions to homework problems for others to use in comparison to their own work. I'm now exploring how to capitalize on the process of students working together during actual class time.

Another thing I noticed on the football field was the relationship between practice and performance. Procedures were learned slowly in practice and gradually improved to the point of rapid and accurate performance (the coach calls it execution) on the day of the game. I recognized that most of my mathematics students grew in ability in the same way. (How could I have been so blind before?) While I continued to have my ever high hopes for them, I came to expect that they would not have much speed or finesse early on. I encouraged them to work toward refined execution so that they would be ready for the big game—uh, the examination.

I also recognized the role played by that ultimate performance, without which practices would lose much of their meaning and purpose. The game, the concert, the play, and the examination are very important as goals and incentives. They provide a focus and a target for students' continually improving efforts. In those highly visible instances, students are on the line. Successful performance is not only a reward in itself, but also an incentive to continue to perform well.

I renewed my efforts to help students succeed. I was less willing to let students fail. I even began to give practice exams when appropriate, just as my colleague coaches staged dress rehearsals and final scrimmages. I began to think of learning and teaching from a new perspective. Again, I sensed that students were responding well. Of course, I recognized that football involves a much larger measure of psychomotor skills than does mathematics, with its heavy focus on cognitive skills. I'm trying to be careful to not overdraw the comparison. But it has been an instructive analogy, and the initial results I have found certainly support its usefulness.

I'm continuing to study my teaching from a coach's perspective, and I expect that I'll discover some other new approaches. I hope so. It's been very satisfying to find that an old teaching dog could learn new tricks.

Can coaching concepts be employed in other academic fields? I think so; they involve some fundamental learning principles. Some of my colleagues in English and in foreign languages are doing so with success, so I suspect that what I learned from the coaches has fairly wide applicability.

Last Saturday, the football team lost rather badly. I came up with several ideas on how the game could have been handled better. I'm waiting for the coach to drop by my office and ask me for some advice—I owe him one.

┌─ Response ──────────────────────────────────┐
│   │
│   │
│   │
│   │
│   │
│   │
│   │
│   │
│   │
│   │
│   │
│   │
│   │
└───┘

2

The Practice of Teaching

Teaching is a profession, just as law and medicine are professions. Should we not, then, speak of "the practice of teaching"? And should not we teachers actually engage in practice?

When I was quite young, I wondered about expressions such as "the practice of law" and "the practice of medicine." The thought of a physician using me to learn diagnostic and treatment skills was a bit unnerving.

Later on, I came to realize that these traditional professions used the term "practice" to designate their activity in the sense of both *applying* skills and knowledge and continually *improving* them through experience. I was considerably relieved.

It occurs to me that teaching is considered a profession for many of the same reasons that law and medicine are considered professions. Why, then, do we not speak of "the *practice* of teaching"?

Surely we teachers apply both knowledge of our special fields and the skills of teaching. Surely we benefit from experience by continually refining our skills in the classroom. We reflect upon a segment of instruction that has gone particularly well, examine why, and try to replicate that performance in the future. Similarly, we look back upon a segment of instruction that has not gone well, examine why, and try to determine modifications; we study our errors and try to reframe them into improved performance in the future. These behaviors would seem to be marks of professional educators.

A teacher sometimes may try a new classroom idea or behavior and find that it doesn't result in immediate success.

It's easy to become discouraged and discard the innovation. However, we should remember that most new things require repeated trials, each in turn coming closer to ideal execution. *Practice* is the handmaiden of successful innovation.

But *practice* has still another sense in teaching. The story is told of a person walking down a New York street carrying a tuba; he asks a newspaper vendor, "Can you tell me how to get to Carnegie Hall?" After eyeing the tuba carefully, the vendor replies, "Practice, man, practice!" Musicians and actors require extensive rehearsal in order to perform well. Athletes do not excel without practice. Teams do not execute plays well without practice. I urge my math students to practice problem-solving techniques in order to achieve competency.

Why should it be any different for teachers? Practice enhances our teaching effectiveness. To neglect it is to risk not becoming all that we can be.

Practice in teaching involves more than just advance trials of classroom exercises and demonstrations. It also involves things such as vocal preparation, rehearsal of movement, and refinement of timing. It involves studying of instructional game plans, including quick mental run-throughs just before class in order to fix those plans in mind. And it is of advantage to get into character, warm-up our voices, and limber up our bodies before entering the classroom—our own special arena of performance.

Does practice make perfect, as we so often hear? Perhaps. But let us realize that perfection is rarely attained even under the best of circumstances. Not achieving that ultimate end can be disheartening. We might better set our eyes on a more realistic objective: continual improvement. John Dewey seemed to have the right words for it: Not perfection as a final goal, but the ever-enduring process of perfecting, maturing, refining, is the aim of living.

And of teaching, I'm sure he would add.

Response

3

Getting a Class to Jell

Suddenly there comes a day when one is conscious that the wariness of strangers thrust together by the vagaries of registration has eased. Students and teacher begin to work together toward a common goal.

I've long been aware of a process that seems to occur in almost every course I teach. For lack of a better term, I've called it jelling.

Suddenly there comes a day when one is conscious that the wariness of strangers thrust together by the vagaries of registration has eased. Students and teacher begin to work toward a common goal. They become comfortable with each other. Students begin to ask questions spontaneously. They respond more readily to teacher queries. It's a moment that arrives without fanfare, and when it does a good feeling develops. Much more importantly, learning is enhanced. The course is on a roll.

I'm sure a lot of teachers encounter similar experiences.

Jelling often manifests itself about a third of the way through the term. When it shows up earlier, I'm delighted. When it's delayed, I'm frustrated. On the rare occasions when it doesn't occur at all, I'm devastated; both students and I hang on for dear life, hardly able to wait until the parting of our ways—all of us are thankful that the academic calendar provides an honorable no-fault means for severing our unproductive and apparently incompatible relationship.

Until recently, I thought that the jelling process was a group phenomenon—the class comes, though perhaps not consciously, to some sort of common sense of moving forward together. But my friend Rebekah Womack suggests an alternative: what I've termed jelling may be a composite of individual processes that she calls bonding, a natural process that can occur between one student and the instructor. In an article, "Of Student Bondage: A Poke at Professional Distance," she says, "[Bonding] isn't quite so tender as what occurs between parent and child in moments following labor and delivery. But it has its own transient wonder. It isn't superglue. But it's strong enough to cement an alliance for a semester."

How does the academic bonding process begin? What conditions foster it? Rebekah thinks that often it is initiated when an instructor is able to call a student by name; that's one early indication of recognizing and respecting a student's individual identity. Bonding continues to build through brief conversations with a student before or after class, or by a chance meeting in the corridor. I find it supported when I provide students with useful pointers on how to deal efficiently and effectively with course material. I often distribute and discuss a one-page summary of these, "How to Succeed in Mathematics with the Least Amount of Effort." (That title, of course, is calculated to draw immediate attention; students soon get to the part that emphasizes that a lot of effort, applied wisely, is still required.) Bonding intensifies during the give-and-take of working one-on-one in office conferences.

Usually I take the time on the second or third day of a course, after enrollment has stabilized a bit, to go through an introduction exercise. Students chat in small groups and then introduce each other to the rest of the class, telling some interesting thing about that person. I'll admit that it's an unusual process to undertake in a math class, but I find that it puts all students more at ease, increases their willingness to speak out and contribute in class, helps all of us to call each other by name, and ultimately leads to enhanced learning.

Bonding is nurtured by finding things of common interest between student and instructor. Sometimes this can be a matter as simple as reading students' T-shirts. "Ah, Popo Agie University—are you from Lander, or have you traveled in Wyoming recently?" I ask a student sporting a shirt emblazoned with a university seal and a moose. She responds, and we are off and running in a conversation about hiking and camping in the Wind River Mountains.

It helps to be somewhat familiar with the territory from which students come. "Jeff Amburgey," I call from the roster on the first day of class; "Are you from the Montgomery County Amburgeys or the Knott County Amburgeys?" It turns out to be Knott County, and we take the conversation to Carr Creek, then up Wolfpen and Dead Mare Branches and finally discover that I've stayed overnight in his great-grandfather's log house. (Sometimes it's hard to contain the conversation—I want to say to him, "I reckon you've seen that ol' black hat hangin' in the loft, with what 'pears to be a bullet hole through the crown, ain't ya?")

Bonding often evolves from a willingness of a teacher to disclose things about one's own self and interests. My references to photography, my comparing academic performance with performance in the concert hall or on the gridiron, and my comments on exploring hidden areas in the Red River Gorge all return dividends to me when students here and there pick up on things that match their own interests. It extends our interactions and relationships.

What works against bonding? Maintaining Perfect Professional Distance—PPD, as Rebekah calls it. PPD keeps both physical and mental space between teacher and students; it avoids subjective feelings that detract from uniformity; it "simplifies" the classroom process by restricting it to straightforward instructor-controlled activity. PPD is the intellectual version of Don't-Touch-the-Student. It's the embodiment of the Familiarity-Breeds-Contempt Axiom.

I've been in classrooms where PPD is operant. I'm very uncomfortable. Everything is quite precise and formal. Sure, some learning may be happening, but it just seems kind of strained and sterile.

I've been in situations where a class has jelled, where a lot of bonding has occurred. I'm very comfortable. Students' reactions are often very spontaneous. It's fun. It may not be easier to teach in that environment because of the continual responsive character of the dynamics; controlling teachers don't have that kind of demand placed on them.

In jelled classes, students don't start packing up their books five minutes before the end of the hour. They sometimes exclaim, "This was a really good class!" or "Yes—I *can* do those problems." They linger and talk with other students or with the instructor. And they leave with smiles on their faces.

I think that bonding and jelling are things that happen naturally with students if only given a chance. The teacher can provide the opportunity by establishing personal openness and responsiveness. Given a conducive climate, the students take it from there. To be sure, forcing such a climate won't work very well, and it can even be counter-productive.

I've suggested to Rebekah that the alternative to PPD is ALC—Appropriate Learning Closeness. Establishing ALC is done both one-on-one and with the class as a whole. It varies, of course, according to individual and collective acceptance and response.

I don't encourage bonding because it's comfortable or fun. I encourage it because I think it can be an important condition that enhances student learning. Teachers have to touch students' minds and students' hearts.

Response

4

The Case for Leaving Things Out

Instead of trying to jam everything in, it might be better to focus on how much one dare leave out of instruction.

How will I ever get it all into a 50-minute lecture? How can I cover everything in a 14-week semester? How can we squeeze all that a major needs to know into just four years of college?

Sound familiar? Almost every teacher with a little bit of experience (say, a week or two) will likely recognize these questions.

The ubiquitous rule is: Jam Everything In! I call it the MedFac Syndrome; nearly every medical school professor I have known lives in fear that a physician ten years into practice will encounter something that the professor neglected to teach 'way back in medical school. It can cause a lot of stress on faculty, not to mention a lot of stress on students.

As pervasive as the questions are, I suggest that often they are the wrong questions for faculty members to ask. When designing instruction, we might better ask ourselves: *How much can I or should I leave out?* Now, that's a rather unconventional assertion, and I know you'll insist that I defend it.

Suppose that you are trying to direct a driver from Indianapolis to Lexington. Do you provide a series of aerial photographs, carefully taped together and marked with the route? Of course not; that much detail severely detracts from your purpose. Instead, you provide a map that represents the route in a schematic way. Better still, you take a sheet of paper, sketch on it two lines at right angles to each other, label them I-65 and I-64, and add a couple of arrows along with circles identified as Columbus, Louisville, and Shelbyville to help orient the driver. You make it simple—a guide—at just the right level of abstraction.

Consider that you are producing a videotape to trigger discussion in a course. Do you lay out 15 to 20 minutes of dialogue, starting with an establishing scene and moving carefully step by step to a logical conclusion of the situation? Definitely not—for one reason, 20 minutes of taping costs a bundle. The better strategy is to determine first the ideal *ending* for triggering response in the students. Then think back to the latest point in the situation with which you can open engagingly. Finally, put as little as possible in between to link the opening and ending. You ought to be able to do it in considerably less than three minutes. Think of the money you save! But more important, the incompleteness imposed by succinctness forces the viewers to speculate about the missing data and to become personally involved in the ensuing discussion—which is the prime objective for your videotape.

If you want students to learn problem solving, it doesn't serve your purpose well to present them with every last datum of a case. That's not realistic. Samuel Butler was on target when he said, "Life is the art of drawing sufficient conclusions from insufficient premises." Students have to learn to identify what additional information they need in order to reach a valid solution. Or, they might hypothesize various alternatives, assess the probabilities of these, carry each alternative to a solution, and then make a decision that optimizes the expected value of the outcome. That's what real life usually requires of people—why not let students get some practice doing it?

Get the idea? Once I caught on to the basic concept represented above, I found another handful of reasons for focusing on how much I dare leave out of my teaching, rather than how much I can jam in. And it works wonders in practice.

So why haven't I listed the other reasons? Perhaps you've guessed it: I don't want to preclude the educational value of your discovering them for yourself and gaining the pride of ownership.

Come to think of it, that's yet another good reason for leaving things out!

A Lesson of a Sierra Evening

If a classroom is to become an environment that inspires students to good thoughts and good work, that will be the result of the effort of the teacher.

As I'm writing these particular paragraphs, I'm sitting in our camp in the Sierra Nevada, deep in what John Muir called the University of the Wilderness.

It's a cool mid-summer evening. A few feet away is a swift-flowing stream, but its sound is almost drowned out by the steady swoosh of the wind blowing through the pines towering overhead. Dusk is falling in our narrow canyon, though the sun still tints the tips of the granite peaks standing guard above Lee Vining Creek. The smell of campfires is in the air.

I'm struck by how inspiring this Yosemite environment is, how conducive it is to generating good thoughts, how easily my pen moves across paper.

And then I think of my classroom. It has a sameness with almost all classrooms. Perhaps yours is basically as uninspiring an environment as mine. That's the way many classrooms are. Almost sterile. There's little that we can change physically. We certainly can't move everything to the Sierra, or to the Bitter-root, or to the Cascades (as much as we might like to). There are practically no variables in the typical classroom.

Except the teacher. And the psychological climate that the teacher might be able to generate.

If a classroom is to become an environment that inspires students to good thought and good work, that has to be the result of a human element—the effort of the teacher.

I cannot duplicate in my classroom the environment of the Sierra, but perhaps I can stir my students a bit as the wind stirs the trees. Perhaps I can get them to sparkle as my stream does as it tumbles around boulders and over bedrock. Perhaps I can surround them with positive stimuli that enhance their self-worth and bring out good things in them.

This in no way takes away the true focus of teaching: the learner, who ultimately must do the learning. If anything, it intensifies that focus by nourishing the individual's ability to learn and grow.

Mountains and trees, canyons and streams, cool winds and warm fires produce an atmosphere. We cannot bring the mountains and all to our students, but we can bring a good atmosphere. And together with our students we can produce our own heights.

Response

Selling Scrap and Education

My scrap-dealing cousin sells me a thing or two about teaching.

I've met many scrap dealers in my life and I've come to have high regard for them. My friends in the scrap business are civic-minded and contribute much of themselves to their communities. They are resourceful people who understand ecology and economics. They also are unassuming and unpretentious.

My cousin Ed Mendel deals scrap in Silicon Valley. His "client list" consists of only 20 companies; he picks up their scrap (sorted according to his specifications) and for the service that he provides *he* pays *them*. Ed learned metallurgy on his own so that he could reclaim and sell the gold, silver, platinum and copper in the material. Thus he helps insure that precious and semi-precious metals are conserved, and he makes a comfortable living out of it. That's *smarts* in my book.

So when Ed talks, I listen. That happened over breakfast in Ed's kitchen a couple of summers ago. The conversation turned to his business, and I asked him the secret of his success—what principles he follows in buying and selling "junk."

"First off, don't call it junk," Ed quickly and kindly corrected me. "Junk has no value. Scrap is something that's left over. It may not be worth much to the person who has it, but it has value for someone. I'm not a junkman; I'm a scrapologist," he said, a twinkle in his eye.

(As I absorbed that little lesson, a vision of my study flashed through my mind. I made a mental note to apply Ed's distinction to the accumulations that had built up in it over the years.)

My cousin continued: "To be a good scrap dealer, you have to be honest in selling your services or your product. You can't just be interested in making the deal and taking away your bucks. You have to have a genuine concern for being of service to the customer."

I found that refreshing, and I asked further what three or four things were characteristic of such sales.

"Number one, you've got to know your product—and be enthusiastic about it," Ed said. "Nothing will kill you quicker than being caught up short about what you're trying to sell. And don't try to fake it; most customers can sniff out a cover-up immediately."

"Second—though maybe as important as the first—you've got to *sell yourself* before you can sell the service or the product."

That was a new idea for me. I asked him what he meant.

"Selling yourself is establishing a positive relationship with the customer, talking on the same wave-length, thinking in the same direction—and, above all, gaining the confidence and trust of the customer. Without that credibility, you and your sale are dead, too."

I nodded understanding. "Please go on," I said.

"And third, the decision to buy is strictly the customer's—not yours. It doesn't do any good to force a sale that's going to result in dissatisfaction. All that stuff that you hear about closing the sale is crap. You're providing a service. You're there to produce happy customers who have made sound decisions about buying into the deal."

Ed paused. He seemed to be studying my face.

"What's the matter?" he asked. "You're frowning. Don't you agree with me? You don't have to…"

"No, I *do* agree with you, but I'm puzzled," I replied. "You don't seem to do much *selling*; you just seem to let the customer do the buying."

"Ah!" he said, his eyes lighting up. "That's where the fourth rule comes in: The seller has to come in at just the right times with the right information to help the customer move to a decision. The timing is really crucial."

It made good sense to me, and I felt my brow relaxing. But suddenly my frown seemed to be transferred to Ed's face.

"Now *you* look puzzled, Ed," I said. "What's troubling you?"

"Well, I *am* puzzled," he replied. "Look, I'm just a scrap dealer, and you're a professor. How come you don't know all this stuff—about knowing the product, selling yourself, and all that? Isn't that what you do all the time in teaching? Don't you have to know your subject, don't you have to convince students of your integrity and gain their trust, don't you have to give them freedom and responsibility to learn for themselves, don't you have to know when to butt in and when to butt out? Isn't the most important thing that you *care* for your students, just as I care for my clients?"

As Ed saw the look of realization spread over my face, he smiled. His questions became rhetorical.

The key principles in selling services and scrap—or anything, for that matter—are the same key principles in my business, selling education to students. I knew that, but I don't think I fully understood it until my scrap-dealing cousin sold me on it.

┌─ Response ───┐
│   │
│   │
│   │
│   │
│   │
│   │
│   │
│   │
│   │
│   │
│   │
│   │
│   │
│   │
└──┘

7

The Legacy of Gus Mueller

What a student taught a teacher about the first day of class.

I don't really remember that very first day of class. I was probably nervous and somewhat discombobulated, being a young and very green TF. (In olden days, graduate students in servitude who toiled in the galleys of introductory courses were called teaching fellows, rather than teaching assistants.) I was facing my first college class. I'm sure, however, that I wanted to make a good first impression.

No, I don't remember that first day, nor do I really remember much of that first semester, years and years ago. What I do remember very well, however, is reading the course evaluations that I had the good sense to ask students to complete at term's end. It was *then* that I learned what kind of impression I made on Day One.

In particular, I remember very vividly what one student, Gustave Mueller, said about that first day (Gus chose to sign his name to the evaluation). At the bottom of the form was scrawled this:

> *When you walked into class the first day, took off your coat and tie, and rolled up your sleeves—I knew it was going to be HELL!*

I did not forget what Gus Mueller said, and I hope I never will. Gus taught me in a very dramatic way the importance of the first day of that course and of any course. What had I communicated when I took off my coat and tie, rolled up my sleeves, and went to work on Gus Mueller's first day in College Algebra? That the course was going to be informal? That I had high expectations for students? That the course was going to be hard work? That we were going to battle over the material? That it was going to be hell, in capital letters?

I probably communicated different things to different students. It may not have been what I intended to communicate. I may not have had *any* deliberate intentions at all when I walked into that classroom on the first day. Maybe it was all an accident—I just did what I did, and it happened to turn out a certain way.

I've thought about this a lot over the years. I think about it especially at the beginning of a new year or a new term. I ask myself: What are the most important things that I want to communicate to this new bunch of Gus Muellers; what messages do I want them to receive on the first day?—Content? Organization? Attitude? Responsibility? Evaluation? Details? Broad overviews? Whatever it is, I have only 45 or 50 minutes in which to do it.

Clearly, I can't do it all. At most, I can work on accomplishing three or four objectives, so I have to choose carefully. I have to assess what I can do "live" and what I can do by other means. I have to assess what I must do on the first day and what can be put off until the next, or the next after that. I have to assess what is *really* essential.

To be sure, this will vary somewhat from course to course, and it certainly varies from teacher to teacher. Over the years I have settled on these components:

1. A good measure of course content—well-presented, I hope.

2. Activity to establish rapport with students, particularly things that communicate that students will be treated as individuals.

3. Participation and involvement by as many students as possible.

4. A sense of what the course will be like: organized, perhaps exciting, work, pretty high expectations, student responsibility.

I'm sure that the choice of other teachers would be quite different, but these are what seem to fit me.

Let me start with the last of these, because I usually spend very little time on it. I don't talk about how the course is conducted. I don't explain the evaluation system. I don't relate how many "cuts" a student is entitled to (none, for my courses). Is this neglect of a fundamental responsibility to students, neglect of a procedure that all deans and the ombudsman strongly recommend? Not at all. I do communicate information on these things (and a lot more) through a rather extensive course description. I distribute it at just about the end of the first class; that way, reading it doesn't divert students from attending to other things I program into my initial meeting with them.

I follow up that description with some commentary and elaboration during the first week or so of the course, but I don't spend a lot of time on it on any given day, especially the first. Further, I want students to realize that some things they must gain from reading, rather than from my presentation. Sometimes I even give a five-minute quiz on the syllabus—not graded, of course—to reinforce the importance of this concept.

I communicate organization and planning primarily by example. What I do in class, even on the first day (*especially* on the first day), reflects that the course is not just "happening." I have a plan and I work toward accomplishing it. But I also allow flexibility to adjust it if learning considerations seem to indicate modifications.

I communicate assignments in writing for two or three weeks in advance so that students *also* can plan their efforts. Even though I have blocked out the course carefully in advance, I don't give assignments for the entire course at the beginning; I want to be able to adjust to circumstances I may discover along the way as the course evolves.

Because I communicate by means of the course description, the first assignment sheet, and the way I personally function, I don't really devote any extensive time on the first class day to my organization and planning objective. Nevertheless, I think I get it across quite well.

I begin to establish rapport even *before* the first class begins. Some students always arrive early for class, and I do too. We chat informally. I begin to check the class list. My having looked over the roster in advance in order to become familiar with names and to work on special pronunciations makes it easier to associate a lot of names with faces even on the first day. I find that it goes quickest with those who sit in the far corners and those with special visual features. If I'm doing well, I can call by name several students in different parts of the room by the time the first class actually begins.

For those who arrive at the bell, it must look like I know everyone right away. I don't, of course, but I work on it diligently over the next few days. It's one of those things that helps students feel that they'll be treated as individuals.

Pre-class conversation with students helps establish an important pattern of student response. There are several ways to engage students in casual conversation. One I like to use when possible is reading and responding to T-shirts. It sounds a little crazy, but it works: "Florida—were you a student there or is Florida your home?" "Popo Agie University? You must be from pretty close to Lander, Wyoming, right?" They relax and they respond. Even more importantly, right from the start I engage students in dialogue about course material. The pattern I set the first day—properly reinforced, of course—will persist throughout the term.

It is my content objective that occupies the most time on the first day—over half the class period—and requires the most preparation. I firmly believe that if I can accomplish only one thing in the first class meeting it must be to convey to the students *something of value* about the course. The content portion of my first class is probably my most carefully designed learning segment of the entire course.

Seldom does first-day content deal directly with Chapter I, Section 1, of the text. (Often students can handle that on their own, without my mediation.) The material has to be of consequence; it has to be representative of the course. It not only has to captivate students, but it must also engage them in the process of learning—actively and immediately. That's no small order!

In Introductory Statistics, I often bring in the latest poll on political candidates or reports on research that involve statistics. We consider how the inferences are drawn from a sample, whether or not the conclusions are to be believed, and what further information we need to know in order to establish validity. I may conduct an on-the-spot survey in the class and examine the extent to which we can draw inferences from it. Sometimes I get a volunteer group to come forward and in a matter of moments they become data in a rank-order correlation exercise which examines in a very visible way the relationship between height, weight, and other variables [see "Students Become Data—Statistics Comes Alive," Chapter 20]. We get a solid feel for the experience of statistics, even though an indepth treatment of these topics will not come for several weeks.

In Calculus I, I'm likely to program into the first class a consideration of how to approximate the area of a geometric region by breaking it up into smaller regions, approximating their areas, and then summing to get the total area. By finer subdividing, better approximations are obtained, which leads to a general consideration of how variable quantities may approach some fixed value, a "limit." By asking appropriate questions, I can get students to develop the concepts themselves. They find that they are *doing* calculus, not just reading about it. They find that it is not impossibly difficult and that it might even be exciting. This is not likely to be the case if we spend our time on the first day reviewing the definition of "function" and finding limits of simple functions out of context.

On the first day in a graduate course on college teaching, I trigger discussion on expectations communicated on the first day with a short, provocative film of an instructor trying to communicate *his* expectations on the first day of class. We go from there to discover that expectations reflect not only the objectives but also a philosophy of instruction, thereby laying the foundations for the next several seminars.

Certainly, the selection of format and materials for the initial meeting with students is a function of the course, the students, and the instructor's goals. Over the years I have developed activities that have worked for me; other combinations may work better for other instructors. The first day is the optimal time in the course to begin establishing attitudes, patterns, expectations, and rapport. To simply pass out a syllabus, take attendance, give an assignment, and dismiss students is missing a tremendous opportunity.

So, I owe a lot to Gustave Mueller, who taught me that. By virtue of his having a significant influence on my teaching for many years, he would qualify as one of my mentors, even though he was a student at the time, back in those halcyon Wisconsin days. I want to express my appreciation to him for this legacy. Unfortunately, over the years I've lost track of him. Thus, I'm taking this public means of saying, "Thank you, Gus Mueller, wherever you are." Maybe it will put us in touch once again.

┌─ Response ─────────────────────────────────────┐
│   │
│   │
│   │
│   │
│   │
│   │
│   │
│   │
│   │
│   │
│   │
│   │
└──┘

8

Students as Scrambled Eggs and Other Recipes for Teaching

Cooking experiences stir up some recipes
for savorous teaching.

I was standing in the kitchen, preparing breakfast for our overnight guests. Gary slipped up behind me, observed for a moment, and said, "You're bringing those eggs along very nicely..."

"Just like students," I replied, almost without thinking.

"What do you mean?" Gary asked.

"Well, you have to apply just the right amount of heat and stir them intermittently and gently—otherwise you get an omelet. And you don't let them get completely done in the skillet; turn them out on the plate at the right time and let the heat within them continue the process," I said, warming to the topic.

The amusement showing on Gary's face only spurred me to continue.

"It's not just the teaching—uh, cooking process, either. You don't just drop the eggs into the pan, cook them for three hours, and eat them with salt and pepper (shells and all), as a first-grader might prescribe. First, you crack them into a bowl, add just a bit of salt to help break down the albumen, add milk if you wish, then beat them to an appropriate state of uniformity."

Thus was born the idea of students as scrambled eggs. It was one of those rare instances where one's subconscious produces a spontaneous response that lingers on to acquire considerable significance. The more I reflected on that morning in the kitchen, the more my mind conjured up cooking metaphors for teaching.

I treated some of my students as roast prime rib. I applied a lot of heat for a short period of time at the beginning in order to seal in the juices. Then I reduced the temperature to about 275 degrees and completed the process slowly, ensuring a high degree of tenderness.

There's room for creativity in teaching as well as in cooking. Just as I introduced a delightful tartness to apple pie by including a generous portion of cranberries to the filling, on occasion I introduced a new ingredient into the classroom—always making sure to balance creativity with judgment. My willingness to innovate in the kitchen encouraged me to innovate in the classroom. The students ate it up.

Often I found that the inclusion of one additional ingredient became the critical element which turned an everyday dining (learning) experience into a very special occasion. Just as a touch of allspice "made" my several cream cheese spreads for apples, I spiced my classes with the unexpected ingredient. For example, in probability demonstrations, instead of using dice I used astragali (sheep heel bones), the original "bones" used by ancient Egyptian gamblers. (Being on good terms with the local butcher comes in handy in a lot of ways.)

New and unlikely combinations sometimes produce tasty dishes. Inspired by a mundane peanut butter and celery snack, I developed a dip for fresh vegetables made from sour cream and peanut butter, augmented with crumbled bacon, minced onions, and other appropriate flavors—it has become a classic. My newfound creative courage in cooking extended to the classroom, where, for example, I mixed a Carnac-the-Magnificent act with calculus to illustrate that integration could be considered a matter of finding the questions to which the derivative was the answer.

In the kitchen, there were times when I had to substitute ingredients. Having no ground almonds or Mexican chocolaté, I used peanut butter and unsweetened cocoa to turn my sauce for chicken into a respectable molé. Having no tart apples, I made an outstanding Dutch apple pie from green tomatoes. Likewise, in the classroom, I used jars of M&Ms in a sampling distribution experiment when I could not afford a standard set of colored marbles. (And the students were able to consume the data at the end of the experiment!)

For a long time I pondered about my associating food with teaching, two things which do not seem to have a natural relationship. Finally, it dawned on me one morning at breakfast: teaching and food are the two primary things that provide sustenance for a teacher. From food we get energy and satisfaction. No less do we draw energy and satisfaction from teaching. What teacher has not experienced that vibrancy of excitement, euphoria, and joy at the end of a class that has gone particularly well? That's what keeps us striving toward excellence.

Furthermore, producing a good meal involves blending ingredients, contrasting sweet and sour, timing, and attending to arrangements of elements (including presentation to the diner). All these considerations are part of the creative process of teaching, too.

Well, the analogies between kitchen and classroom kept coming to mind—many more than I report here. Once I got started on it, I couldn't seem to think of anything else. Then one day I got to talking over the fence to my neighbor about it. He looked up from his gardening with a perverse twinkle in his eye.

"Now that you've mastered the art of how to cook students, do you suppose you could turn things around and think about how to teach vegetables?" he asked, in deadpan seriousness.

That broke the spell. I am no longer obsessed with the cooking-teaching metaphor. But I'm still willing to share a few academic recipes with my friends so that they, too, may savor the results of creative efforts in both kitchen and classroom.

9

What Heisenberg Might Say About College Teaching

We must deal with the uncertainty principle in teaching as well as in physics.

Thanks to Stephen Hawking's unlikely best-seller, *A Brief History of Time,* Heisenberg is back into public consciousness. Heisenberg, Werner Heisenberg—you know, the scientist who first presented the uncertainty principle and revolutionized thinking in atomic physics back in the 20s and 30s.

Heisenberg posited that the very attempts to measure the position or velocity of a particle affected that position and velocity. Or, stated another way, one cannot measure both the position and velocity with accuracy. That is, attempts to measure affect the measurement.

If Heisenberg were alive today, he'd roll over in his grave at our attempts to assess teaching effectiveness through classroom observation.

Indeed, almost any student in elementary physics would detect flaws in the process that is becoming commonplace in evaluation for promotion and salary advancement in colleges and universities. What would appall the physics student is that the classroom evaluation process usually draws conclusions from only a single observation. Doing that in a physics experiment would rate a cold F.

Heisenberg might say that the presence of the observer affects the behavior being observed. Teachers will prepare better for classes that they know will be observed. (And it's unconscionable to do observations without advance announcement.) Teachers will pull out all their best classroom tricks for the observer. They'll try to play heavily into any known biases of the observer. After all, teachers are human.

Students, too, are human. They act differently when an observer is present; often they respond in ways to make the teacher look good. And the entire atmosphere can be charged with a tension that is not there normally.

I recall one memorable instance of my being observed (with less than 30-minute notice) by my division chair, a scientist who himself had a reputation among students as being a mean teacher (that was not "mean" in the statistical sense, either). He entered my class late, departed early, and later declared that he hadn't noticed that the students reacted any differently while he was there. The "well-above-average" evaluation that I received as a result certainly did nothing to build my confidence in the usefulness and validity of the process.

Well, then, should classroom observation be discarded in summative teacher evaluations? Not at all. It focuses on a key dimension of faculty performance, and it still *can* be one of the better options we have available. But it needs to be made more valid.

How? I don't have the definitive, comprehensive answer for that, but here are a few suggestions for starters:

- Make classroom observations more common so that teachers get used to having other non-students in the room. (Benefits might also derive from teachers observing each other frequently—picking up good teaching ideas from each other—without any evaluative overtones.)

- Base evaluation on multiple observations, sampling in different courses and under a variety of circumstances, rather than just observing one instance. Use of two or more observers can help.

- Conduct "trial" observations that aren't recorded and allow the teacher time to improve possible deficiencies prior to an "official" observation. Provide a program that can assist that improvement. (My friend Howard Altman puts it thusly: Development without evaluation is futile, but evaluation without development is fatal.)

- Use checklists that emphasize *descriptions* of behavior, rather than judgments.

- Prior to observation, provide opportunity for teacher and observer to discuss the particular class, its objectives, the students, and their characteristics. Following observation, provide opportunity for the teacher to respond to the observer's conclusions.

- Use observers who themselves are good teachers who thoroughly understand the teaching-learning process. Use observers—perhaps from a different department, division or college—who are not likely to show bias or partiality. If possible, use observers who are especially versed and/or trained in the teaching observation process.

- Mix classroom observation with several other means of evaluation, including teacher self-evaluation.

The key principles operative in the above strategies are to reduce the anxiety attendant to observation and to increase the trust in the observer and the process. An important part of that is to actively involve the teacher in the process—the teacher and observer become collaborators, instead of antagonists.

It should be noted that I'm speaking of summative programs, those designed to make decisions about a teacher's career. *Formative* programs, designed to improve teaching performance, are separate entities. However, successful formative programs are characterized by many of the principles and strategies I have suggested.

Are these suggestions too costly or too time-consuming? I think not. Just as anything worth doing is worth evaluating, anything worth evaluating is worth evaluating correctly. And decisions about a person's career are at least as important and critical as decisions about atomic particles. Let's do them both well.

Would Werner Heisenberg be satisfied with such precautions? Maybe, maybe not. But he certainly would have approved of attempts to reduce the uncertainty in evaluation.

```
┌─ Response ─────────────────────────────────┐
│                                            │
│                                            │
│                                            │
│                                            │
│                                            │
│                                            │
│                                            │
│                                            │
│                                            │
│                                            │
│                                            │
│                                            │
└────────────────────────────────────────────┘
```

10

Future Stuff
for College Teaching

*Technology could enhance student learning and
reduce much of the drudgery of instructional
activity. Will it displace live teachers?*

The coming of the 90s has sparked a wildfire of forward-looking. Almost everyone has become a prophet. *Megatrends* has taken a 10-year leap. And Malcolm Abrams and Harriett Bernstein catalog for us *Future Stuff*, technological developments that are just around the corner.

Some of what Abrams and Bernstein describe is almost here—four-wheel steering on motor vehicles, electronic still photography, voice-activated typewriters, for example. One development is surely to be greeted with great joy: the self-weeding lawn. But some, like the walking desk, an elevated work station mounted over a treadmill so that one can exercise while working, are not likely to become widely popular. And I can certainly do without the "intelligent toilet" (and this article can certainly do without a description of it, but you could look it up if you're really interested—p. 42).

Well, one evening last winter when I was sitting in front of a cheery fire with not a whole lot to do, I got to thinking about Future Stuff. My mind began to wander to college teaching and what technological Stuff might be in its Future—say, by the year 2000 or perhaps 2010, when I might be ready to hang up my academic spurs for the very last time. It's amazing what strange and interesting things can spring from idle minds! (I suppress the impulse to say *bizarre*, but I know what you're thinking.)

While some of what follows has resulted from conversations with friends subsequent to that night, I'll be quick to point out that the responsibility for presentation of ideas here is strictly my own. Even the guilty must be protected in some circumstances.

First off, here's everyone's favorite: an Intrinsic Motivation Pill for students. The Pill would enhance students' reliance on intrinsic rewards and reduce the need for teachers to accommodate extrinsic motivation via exams and grades. The IMP would be in the form of a time-release capsule, of course, with effects extending over at least a day for each dosage. There might even be an IMP+ gelcap that adds an ingredient to increase participation in the classroom.

Next is an Automated Book Retrieval and Shelving System that can be activated from a catalog terminal. Just enter the call number and a stack-robot quickly finds the book and delivers it to you, already charged out. Return the book to a bin and your account is credited as the system returns the book to its proper address in the stacks. ABRSS would save a lot of time and effort. And fewer books would be lost through misshelving. To accommodate voracious browsers like me, grazing displays could still be maintained in the library lobby. (All of this assumes that books do not become obsolete, a dismal prospect that at least is not in the future that I can foresee.)

The All-Purpose Audio-Visual Console would permit even teachers with zero A-V facility to display images on a permanently installed electronic screen. The Console would accommodate any film, tape or disk input—simply insert a cartridge into the slot in which it fits, and everything else would be automatic. The APAVC could be located anywhere in the classroom and it would be operated by a long-life compact battery (with back-up); there would be no power cords for stumble-bums like me to trip over. APAVC would transmit images on radio frequencies, eliminating the need to darken the room. The top surface of the console would function as a table for more traditional transparency use. With proper design, it would not be necessary for teachers to wear lead aprons.

Perhaps the APAVC is a bit grandiose for the average classroom, even one several years into the future. As for myself,

I'd gladly settle for an intelligent overhead projector—one whose light goes on when a transparency is laid on the light table and goes off when the transparency is removed. At the very least, it would be handy to have a pressure-sensitive switch that could be brushed lightly with the heel of the hand as transparencies are manipulated.

The Voice-Activated Writing Surface (writing surfaces were first known as blackboards) is a superb idea, I think. (I would call it superb even if the idea had not been contributed by my spouse.) It really combines the voice-activated typewriter with the electronic screen of the APAVC. When a teacher gives the command "Now write," everything said thereafter appears on the screen in a neat, legible script. Commanding "Now stop" would stop the writing and return the teacher to an audible-only mode. The VAWS would be self-erasing and self-correcting on command. An auxiliary device would give a printout of anything on the screen, if desired.

Since I'm an inveterate room re-arranger, my personal favorite technological innovation for the future is the Magnetic Classroom Layout Grid. On a small screen at a teacher's home base, simply manipulate icons representing the chairs, tables, desks, and other furniture in the room. When you get the appropriate arrangement, press "enter" and the grid duplicates your plan in the classroom with the magnetized real furniture in a matter of seconds. Then, type in STUDENTS and press "enter" and voila!—the doors open and students come into a room arranged specifically for them and the material of the hour.

Ah, what technology might hold for us! It could enhance student learning and reduce much of the drudgery of instructional activity.

Precedents for high technology in education go back farther than you might think. At the University of Wisconsin in 1862 in a North Hall room (where some 90 years later I would be studying mathematics) John Muir—yes, *the* John Muir—applied his talents to mechanical devices to aid the student. He invented and built a full-size working model of an automatic desk that selected and opened each book in turn for a designated period of time. Then he matched this with a device that each morning awakened him and ejected him from bed upon the rising of the sun. Alas, these items that could be so useful even today never caught on.

In the process of my speculating about technology, a few non-technological ideas surfaced. One seems especially promising: the Variable-Length Semester. We all know that some students who fail in courses might succeed if only they had more time. But the layout of instructional activity follows a cardinal rule: the time it takes to teach anything (and hence to learn anything) is directly proportional to the length of a term. Thus, 14-week semesters generate instructional blocks of 14, 28, 42, 56 or 70 "hours" each, and correspondingly we meet in class from 1 to 5 hours per week. Suppose, however, that each semester had a length that could vary from 12 to 18 weeks. Some students might demonstrate competence in a course at 12 weeks and complete it (maybe taking the next several weeks for independent and supplemental study). Others could take longer, even past the time designated as standard. It's not a perfect procedure, but it does begin to combat the calendar-constraint syndrome that affects much of higher education.

Regrettably, two of the most time-consuming activities of teachers do not seem to lend themselves to the stuff of technology. No doubt you have already guessed what most teachers would like: simplification of the processes of course design and evaluation of students.

It's been suggested that a computer program be developed to lay out the design for a course. Enter all the variables— subject, difficulty-level, course objectives, number of students, level of students, learning style preferences of students, teaching style preferences of teacher, size of room, time of day, etc.—and out pops a full-blown design for the semester. Wishful thinking. Of course it won't work. There are too many variables and they keep changing. Courses are dynamic and they require intricate judgment of the teacher to keep fine-tuning them. This dimension of the teacher's role may represent teaching at its best.

Then there's evaluation. Sure, exams can be constructed from test banks. (I've tried it several times in statistics—with little success.) Self-scoring exams of all sorts have existed for decades. But no scoring program can provide feedback tailored to the specific individual. Only a sensitive and informed teacher can perceive a student's miscues and offer just the right amounts of redirection and encouragement. Again, it's teaching at its best.

So, never fear. Teachers will not be displaced by technology. Rather, whatever technology comes down the pike will likely free teachers for their finest hours. Now, *that* is Stuff of the Future that I really look forward to.

```
┌─ Response ──────────────────────────────────────────┐
│                                                      │
│                                                      │
│                                                      │
│                                                      │
│                                                      │
│                                                      │
│                                                      │
│                                                      │
│                                                      │
│                                                      │
│                                                      │
│                                                      │
│                                                      │
│                                                      │
│                                                      │
└──────────────────────────────────────────────────────┘
```

11

How to Grow Students

Tending a garden requires sensitive monitoring and knowledgeable application. So, too, do our interventions in the learning process.

My neighbor Delmas Crowe is a gardener. A darn good one. Each spring and summer I study his activity across our fence, and I marvel at how good a teacher he could be. Del understands how things grow.

For one thing, he understands that each seed, each plant has a potential to be a certain something. His role as gardener is to see that the potential is realized. He doesn't try to grow beans on tomato vines or squash on corn stalks. At best, each plant can become only what it can be.

Our students, too, have potentials—much more complex than plants, but perhaps just as much genetically determined. Would that we discover their potentials and nurture them. It would save the futility of trying to grow them into something that they cannot be. Would that our students discover what their potentials are. It would help them grow sturdy, to their maximum height, and fully productive.

Another thing that Del understands is that his plants do the growing. The most he can do is help provide favorable conditions for them. He knows what is conducive to their growth: light, water, certain nutrients, the absence of competing weeds. We, too, can provide sustaining elements for our students, but it is still they who must take these elements and do the growing.

Del knows when and how to tend his garden. Too much water will drown his plants; not enough will stunt them. Too much fertilizer will burn them out; too little will make them spindly. Tending a garden requires sensitive monitoring and knowledgeable application. So, too, do our interventions in the learning process.

The aim of both teaching and gardening is to nurture the innate capabilities of the individual.

Neither teaching nor gardening is easy work. But done diligently, both processes bear great fruit—fruit that brings us satisfaction and sustenance beyond compare.

I don't myself cultivate a garden. But I do cultivate my neighbors. Del Crowe is so successful that his harvest runneth over. I reap both from his example and from his garden.

Response

12

How to Prevent Students

Can it be that things one does for students, with all good intentions, actually work against them?

I was relaxed and comfortable, waiting a few minutes more until the anesthesia wore completely off. A bit of casual conversation by the dentist might be appropriate, perhaps even expected after the crown was seated and cemented.

But there was a hesitant tone in Alix's voice: "Do you mind, uh, if I ask you a question?"

"Of course not," I said, reaching over my shoulder to hit the button to tilt up the chair a bit. I'd spent enough time around dentists that I was quite at ease with them, and I had come to know my way around their environment. In fact, some of my best friends are dentists—Alix among them.

"I feel sort of funny asking you this, but we've known each other for a long time..."

True; our friendship went back several years to when Alix was a dental student, and we had kept in close touch after graduation. By now, we were colleague-colleague, rather than student-professor or dentist-patient.

"...Well, you know I've always been tuned in to patient education, and I have a practice that is highly oriented to prevention."

True, again; Alix was a socially sensitive person and had gone to a progressive dental school; I would have expected nothing else.

"But it doesn't always work—I don't seem to be really getting through to some of my patients. They come back for recall, and they're in just as bad a shape as on their previous visit. And a few of them almost seem to resent and resist my efforts."

"I know," I said. "A couple of members of my family may be in that category."

A slight, but knowing smile crossed Alix's face.

"What can I do? How can I get them to cooperate? How can I get them to do what they should do?"

In a moment of minor inspiration, I tilted the chair all the way up, swung my legs to the side, and got up. "Here," I said. "Sit down."

Alix's eyes questioned me.

"Go ahead, sit in the chair," I insisted.

She did, and swung her legs up. I tilted the chair and adjusted it to the appropriately supine treatment position.

"How does it feel," I asked.

"My God!" Alix exclaimed. "I never realized! It's well, it's like I feel so helpless, so out of control, so vulnerable!"

"Do you suppose that may have something to do with your patients' attitudes?"

"Yeah, I never thought of it that way before," she replied. "I'm in charge, and they're subservient. No wonder I have trouble getting them to be responsible for their own health care. How could I do that to them?"

"Let me suggest that you didn't do anything *to* them. Maybe that's just the natural state of affairs between patient and practitioner. Maybe you should focus on what you *haven't* done to *reduce* their depending entirely on you. Your professional knowledge and skill are always going to place some distance between you and your patients; you have to accept that, and it's not all bad, of course. But you might search for alternatives that don't accentuate it and for things that you can do that will help keep it from preventing them from becoming *good* patients."

Alix nodded agreement, tilted the chair, and got up.

We explored the matter further. Another thing that we concluded was that a dentist can do too much for a patient or promise too much—for example, by implying that anything that goes wrong can be "fixed" by the dentist—literally insuring that the patient stays in the dentist's good hands. There is little for the patient to be responsible for; there is little need to care about one's own health. In the name of prevention, the patient has been prevented from becoming a good patient.

Alix and I became so involved in discussing these issues that we ran 'way into her next appointment. She scheduled me for another appointment—wisely for a double one—so that we could continue our exploration of the subject.

When I returned in two weeks, we examined an additional dimension that might lead patients to avoidance behavior with regard to dental care, rather than to approach behavior: the environment of the dental office. Fortunately, there was no inane television set to deal with, but we decided to replace the canned "elevator music" from the local radio station with good tapes carefully selected from Alix's library of recordings. In general, the patient waiting area passed our inspection. A planter that created a minor barrier in front of the receptionist was moved, and a chair was placed in front of the desk for the convenience of patients. The reading material for patients already included an appropriate amount of health information.

Then we considered how Alix and her assistants had been conducting patient education activities. Frequently, conferences with patients were being held at chairside or at a nearby desk. We decided that whenever possible it would be better to carry out this function completely away from the treatment area, at a table where patient and practitioner could sit side by side. The staff also reaffirmed that good communication would be enhanced by their listening attentively to patients' questions and being especially careful to not respond to them prematurely. We even examined how the attire of the staff might affect relationships with patients. Thus we identified a lot of little adjustments that added up to an improved office climate.

When I left Alix's office that day, I felt pretty good. We had discovered a lot that was likely to ameliorate the problem Alix had brought up. I smiled to myself as I anticipated the customary billing that I would get from Alix's office: charges for dental procedures and a final add-on for "preventive dentistry." I mused that maybe I should send her a bill in return, for "preventive education."

However, as I was driving home my pseudo-smugness began to leave me. A nagging set of thoughts began to creep into my head. Alix's question "How can I get my patients to cooperate?" began to translate into my own question: "How can I get my students to cooperate?" Why did I think that her problem with some patients was any different from my problem with some students? How could I get them to work with me rather than resist my efforts? How could I get them to be responsible rather than to be dependent on me? How could I get them to approach learning rather than to avoid it? Could it be that the things Alix and I had worked out for her practice also needed to be applied in my classroom? Could it be that the things I was doing *for* students, with all good intentions, were actually working *against* them?

Had I inadvertently been preventing students—independent, responsible students who exercised initiative for learning—just as Alix had been preventing patients, ironically in the name of prevention itself? It was a sobering thought, and I began to look at my teaching from a new perspective.

Over the years it had become my custom to provide students with a lot of duplicated material: course descriptions, periodic assignment sheets, sample exams, solution sheets after exams, and the like. I re-examined these procedures. Some of the material was distributed in the interests of accuracy and efficiency. On the other hand, when it got down to sample exams, I wondered whether I was doing too much for students. Would they not learn more if they had to review the chapters themselves, infer the relative importance of topics, and organize their own study strategies? Wouldn't it be better if they took this responsibility themselves rather than being dependent on me? Definitely yes, I concluded.

Just before the next examination, I started to work with my students, helping them to organize their review process. By the end of the term I wanted them to be able to do this completely on their own, with my role being reduced to that of a consultant. In another course, I asked the students themselves to design and submit questions that they thought were appropriate for the exam; I used these as the basis for a review during the last class meeting before the test. What were the results? I couldn't tell in any scientific way, of course, but I knew I had made the right moves. Several students confirmed this on the course evaluations.

For a certain chapter in statistics that contained an unusual mass of intricate formulas, I had been giving out "formula sheets" that students could use during examinations. I changed that process to one of allowing students to bring to the exam one note card, 3 inches by 5 inches, containing on one side whatever information they wished. I cautioned them that putting too much information and full problem solutions on the card might be counterproductive; they might not be able to find what they wanted among all the fine printing. Again, this new procedure seemed to work. Students reported that the very process of organizing and preparing the card helped them learn the material. Some used only part of the card. Many reported that they used the card during the exam only as a final confirmation of information they had internalized in preparing the card—it was a check, rather than a crutch.

When students asked me to work a troublesome homework problem in class, I used to jump right into it and efficiently produce an ideal solution. I changed to having other students work the problem or at least make significant contributions to the solution. Sometimes they started to lead me down an unproductive path, but I drew learning out of that, too. The process often took longer, but I felt the results were well worth it, and I adjusted my organization and design of class activity to accommodate it.

Flushed with these successes, I continued to look for ways to wean students from depending on me, and one of my main goals became trying to convert them to responsible, independent learners. One aspect of this was to examine whether I was accenting my authority position too much. To be sure, I *am* the authority, both in knowledge and in controlling the chips—i.e., grades. It would be foolhardy to think that I could mask that fact and the students' perception of it. Even if I could, it would probably be undesirable to do so. But I might be able to remove some of the visible symbols of that authority in order to generate more of a climate of working together. In my office, I moved my desk so that it no longer separated me from the student; we worked together off the end of the desk. Then, I found an even better arrangement: I moved a conference table so that I could easily shift into working side by side whenever a student comes in for help.

In the classroom, I couldn't change from a standing position to a sitting position, given the constant need for board work in my field. However, I made one change that seemed of major significance: I moved the table and lectern from front-and-center to the side of the room. This immediately changed the ambience in the room. Surprisingly, it gave me greater freedom of movement—I no longer had a home base to gravitate back to. I found that taking a position near the ends of the front row seemed to encourage students to participate more in analyzing problems, proposing solutions, and contributing in general to the development of the material. I found that I had to move the table each day before class, because the custodial staff always returned it to the "spot of authority." I didn't mind the small extra effort; now I was defining the climate of the classroom, rather than by default allowing the janitor to do so.

Did my modified classroom behavior work? I think so, although I can offer no data from a controlled experiment to support that contention. I think the response of students was positive, too, as evidenced by comments such as this, made by a student introducing me to his mother: "... he's a professor, but he's... well... he's different! He's always working *with* us."

There were other ways that I tried to adjust the climate of my courses. Taking a cue from Alix, I modified my student conference hours, times when I would definitely be in my office and available for consultation. I knew that students sometimes came by, saw that I was with another student or on the telephone, and then left before I could signal them to wait. Under the new arrangement, I still had definite hours, but I encouraged them to telephone or to see me after class to make an appointment during these times (or at other times, if necessary) in order to not have to wait to see me. The number of conferences increased.

I also tried to arrive early for class and to engage students in informal conversation. I made a point of not doing this from a position in the front of the room; rather, I sat in a seat on the side and varied that position from day to day. I was especially attentive about listening carefully to students.

Well, you get the idea without my citing examples endlessly. By keeping in mind two or three basic principles, I continue to find ways of modifying my approach to students so as to promote their skills in learning. (You notice that I do not now list those principles, as you expected; I want you to look back over what I've said and formulate them for yourself.) I'm trying to be particularly sensitive to things that I might be doing in the guise of helping students that in fact might be preventing them, however subtly, from being *good* students. I'm trying to give them the freedom to learn and grow on their own. It's an exciting endeavor.

Today, I got a bill from Alix's office. The last item on it was the charge that I had come to expect, but this time it was worded "patient education." I wrote out a check immediately and on impulse wrote "tuition" in the space on the lower left. Across the bottom of the statement I wrote "THANKS!" in large letters. And added, "—for helping me learn how to teach students rather than to prevent them." I can't wait 'til my next appointment to tell her all about it!

Response

13

Truckin' and Teachin'

Travelling twenty-five days and eight-thousand-some miles in an eighteen-wheeler produces some lessons that are worth sharing with others.

Last fall I was invited to accompany an over-the-road tractor-trailer driver for a few weeks in order to learn more about her job of trucking. As you might guess, this certainly did not turn out to be your average run-of-the-mill academic investigation.

When I told some of my friends about my forthcoming "research," they were not surprised. "It sounds like something you'd do," one said. "You'll probably figure out some way to turn it into another of your crazy pieces on teaching," added another.

"I hope so," I replied to the latter. "I'll look upon that as a challenge. And you know that I'm not the kind of guy to disappoint my friends."

Hence, this article. Besides, I'm not likely to travel 8,629 miles in an eighteen-wheeler without learning something useful that's worth sharing with others.

When I returned from my 25-day cross-country adventure, my friends asked me what it was like. I told them that trucking was not just the allowable ten hours of driving each day. It was an activity that expanded and consumed almost every minute of my waking hours. (It also consumed all my sleeping hours, which were spent restlessly atop the "doghouse," the housing over the 320HP engine which throbbed beneath me.)

I discovered that trucking requires a surprising amount of detailed planning. It's relatively enjoyable when rolling down the road on a clear day with little traffic. But it's tedious at other times—and downright boring and exasperating when waiting for call-backs from Dispatch. The "good pay" that many people ascribe to trucking is not very good when the long working hours are taken into consideration.

Trucking is hardly a life of free-wheeling independence that some might think. There are frustrating (yet largely necessary) constraints: restricted roads, low clearances, DOT regulations, company policies, and the like. Truckers don't get a lot of respect—sometimes not even from their employers.

"Hmm," my friends said. "It sounds a lot like teaching."

I reported that communication between drivers and the company could be vastly improved. There are many less-than-competent bureaucrats in the company's planning, payroll, and maintenance departments. Often directives are arbitrary. All too few dispatchers and other administrative functionaries have been on the road themselves, so they don't really comprehend the problems of the drivers and the intricacies of meeting delivery schedules. A few simple adjustments, some of them merely common courtesies, on the part of the employer could improve the lot of drivers immensely.

My friends nodded knowingly. "Much like some universities," they said.

I could only smile.

I found a central axiom common to both trucking and teaching: Anticipate. A truck driver is always planning routes, calculating times of transit, and carefully programming stops for fuel, telephone calls, and showers. A good driver is constantly alert to the unseen and unexpected, ready to assess changing circumstances in order to make adjustments— slowing down, speeding up, shifting, maintaining safe distance.

So too in teaching do we have to anticipate the unexpected and take many factors into consideration when we design our activity: the student, the material, the route of delivery, the schedule, our resources. These all are orchestrated toward our ultimate destination: learning. And we must constantly monitor our progress toward that end and make adjustments accordingly. (We may even double-clutch when we have to down-shift.)

Truckers are committed to whatever is necessary to accomplish their job, delivering a load on time. I found that this often required rising early, as well as working late into the night. Sometimes it required skipping meals. Teaching requires similar dedicated behavior in order to fulfill commitments to meet each class fully prepared.

Truckers encounter frustrations daily—ridiculous traffic, aggressive and/or inconsiderate drivers of four-wheelers, "garbage" on the CB. I admired my driver's ability to remain calm in such circumstances; her being able to defer expression of anger reduced the risks that could be incurred through impulsive reactions. In teaching, too, calm equanimity serves well in the face of frustrating classroom situations.

Both truckers and teachers perform important functions in our society but often are not recognized for their significant contributions. Not all of us can achieve Great Things in our lives. I'm reminded of Helen Keller's comment, "I long to accomplish a great and noble task, but it is my chief duty to accomplish humble tasks as though they were great and noble. The world is moved along not only by the mighty shoves of its heroes, but also by the aggregate of the tiny pushes of each honest worker."

Truckers are among the honest workers who help move the world along. So are teachers. I have come to admire both truckers and teachers for fulfilling useful roles in our society, often performing work that is not easy. I admire them for their persistence in the face of less-than-ideal circumstances for carrying out their responsibilities.

I especially admire my daughter, the trucker who provided me the opportunity to learn some new lessons and relearn some old lessons about life and work and the dignity of both. In that sense, she was both trucker and teacher.

My trucking odyssey was a wonderful, fascinating, and productive experience. The lessons within it can serve well, whether we keep on truckin' or keep on teachin'.

14

If Football Were Played by Math Students...

*When the coach called for volunteers from the
student body, ten of my math students responded.
I was pleased; I hoped that my students would
introduce some rational problem solving to the
gridiron. But I was surprised by the coach's phone
call three weeks later.*

It was the stuff of an academic nightmare!

Due to very unusual circumstances that perhaps are best
left unmentioned here, a sizeable portion of our football team
was declared "no longer eligible for competition" after the first
game of the season. Both assistant coaches were relieved of
their responsibilities. The alumni were in an uproar. The coach
was distraught. The comptroller, eyeing her balance sheets,
was quietly apprehensive. The campus was in turmoil.

While various appeals were filed (none was to be successful),
the coach put out an urgent call for volunteers from the student
body. Every walk-on would be given a fair opportunity to make
the team—and being able to *walk* on was the first criterion. I
was surprised and inwardly pleased when ten students from
my introductory math courses responded to the call to school
spirit and patriotic duty. I was certainly doing my part in
contributing to the old college try. Math does more than its
share, I gloated to myself. Maybe my students will introduce
some rational problem solving to the gridiron, I hoped.

I was not at all prepared for the phone call that came early one evening about three weeks later.

"Prof, this is Coach Rice," shouted the voice at the other end.

I didn't have time to respond before it continued: "Prof, what in *the* H are you doing to those students over there? Just what is going on in those classrooms? I simply can't believe it!" the voice sputtered.

I squeezed in a couple of words, "Why, Coach, what do you mean?"

"What do I mean? It's those math students you sent me. What are you doing to them? They're really screwed up…"

I sent them I thought as he raced on; they're only volunteers.

"…How am I supposed to field a team with people like that? I've never seen such a bunch of crazy attitudes!"

I put on my best nondirective voice in an attempt to calm him: "Gee, Coach, could you give me an example?"

It didn't work. "An example, an example!" he shouted all the louder, "I'll give you a dozen examples, two dozen—a hundred! Take that Jankowich…"

Nice kid, I thought, made an A in pre-calc.

"…He missed practice last week because he had to help his girlfriend move. And he missed again on Monday because he had a dental appointment—'They're hard to get,' he tells me."

All I could say at that point was a quiet, "Hmm."

"Last Saturday I had to put Wilson in at quarterback. The second play I sent in, he called time-out. He told me he learned the play for the previous game, but he didn't know he'd have to use it again this week. He asked me to sketch it out for him one more time."

Coach went on and on. One player didn't get his weight work in for three days, then wanted to make it all up in five hours on Thursday. Another waited until the night before the game to study the playbook so that everything would be fresh in his mind for the game. Players wanted the coach to demonstrate the plays over and over but didn't want to run through them themselves. Coach didn't give a hundred examples, but I'll bet he was well beyond two dozen.

"And the crowning blow was at the end of practice tonight— three of your math players came up to me and asked if I could postpone the game until next Wednesday; they thought they could perform a lot better if they had three more days to practice!"

By now, I had begun to realize what he was facing; it was the same thing I ran into in the classroom rather frequently. Being just a bit amused at the carry-over to football, I couldn't resist asking him whether anyone reported that his dog ate the playbook.

"No, it was a cat, not a dog," he replied, "And it didn't eat the book, it—er—well, never mind!"

Finally I said, "Well, Coach, I hear what you're saying, but what am I supposed to do about it?"

He was quick to respond: "You professors are supposed to build some character in those kids. Make them take responsibility. Teach them the importance of commitment. Hold some expectations for them. Use positive reinforcement. Extinguish negative behavior. And get them to realize that it takes practice and hard work in order to succeed. You guys in the classroom should know all that."

"Now, look, Coach," I replied. "My job is to teach my subject. It's the students' choice whether they do the things to learn it; I can't force them. They pay their money; they decide whether to get their money's worth."

Coach came back at me sharply: "Prof, do you think I could field a team that way? Do you think I could win games? I can't be laissez-faire about it. How long do you think I could keep my job if I looked at things that way?"

I began to wonder whether he had a point there. "Tell you what, Coach," I said, remembering my long-grown-cold supper, "I'll drop around to see you tomorrow afternoon; let's talk about it more."

We did that the next day—and several more times as the season advanced. We exchanged ideas on teaching and began to understand each others' points of view. We found that we agreed on more things than we had realized before. We became good friends.

Fast-forward now to November—to the final game of the season with arch-rival Tech. Our team had managed to put together a 5-5 record. Winning this last one meant a winning season, despite all the hardships. Coach had invited me to sit right behind the bench for this noble final effort.

Now it's the final quarter, less than three minutes to go, and the score is tied at 23-all. Tech has the ball and is driving steadily down the field. Suddenly, Jankowich intercepts a pass and runs it all the way back to the Tech 28-yard line! We have a chance to win if we play it right! Our players are jumping up and down. Wilson leads the offensive team back onto the field. The crowd goes wild!

But then the noise dwindles to a hush. Everyone is looking at a small group of players clustered on our sideline. Someone is lying on the field. I walk over—it's Coach Rice! He was swept over by the swarm of Tech players who were desperately trying to force Jankowich out of bounds.

The trainer and I kneel at Coach's side. He's barely conscious. It's probably a concussion. A stretcher is brought out. Just before he's taken off the field, Coach looks up and grasps the front of my jacket.

"Take over, Prof," he croaks, "You can do it; we can win."

They carry him away. I'm still kneeling on the sideline. My head is whirling. I break out in a cold sweat. The referee is blowing his whistle.

I can't seem to move from my kneeling position. I twist and turn. It's unreal. I keep trying to claw my way out of the turmoil. Things fade in and out of focus. It seems to go on for an eternity.

Suddenly, everything becomes still, except for the pounding of my heart. I try to convince myself that I'm awake. I shiver and pull the clammy covers up around my neck. My mind races.

It *has* all been a dream! It's not the Tech game. Coach hasn't designated me to take over. My math students aren't playing football. It's not November. It's only September, and I'm lying scrunched down in my bed, trying to erase all those vivid images.

Trouble is, I can't erase them. They continue to haunt me. I get up and brew some coffee. I sit down at the typewriter and begin to peck out this strange story.

It's only September. The semester's barely begun. I still have a good shot at my math students. I can communicate ever higher expectations for them. I can try to get the Jankowiches committed to giving academics their highest priority, working other things around their school responsibilities. I can try to teach the Wilsons that everything is important—it's all interrelated and it all fits together.

I don't have to accept my students' "crazy attitudes," as Coach Rice called them. I can do all the things that Coach does to insure high performance. I can convince my charges that they can't slide through training, and I can convince them that it takes steady, consistent effort if they are to execute plays with precision and succeed on the field, in the classroom, in life.

I don't know about "character," but I may even work a little bit on that, too.

I've decided that in my classes we don't have to run the semester right down to the wire, with students hoping to luck out at the end. We can make it a winning season right from the start!

Response

15

Yet Another Voice on Educational Reform

Alkschmeer's Geographic Quotient is a little known concept, but it holds as much water as many solutions for school improvement currently being pushed.

Jake, the bartender, and I were having another of our philosophical discussions, it being a pretty slow evening at the Keeneland Oasis. As usual, we had finally gotten around to education—this time that report about how school systems in other countries were beating the pants off ours because kids were in school longer and all that.

Jake's a pretty good authority on the underside of education, having turned to a more lucrative profession after being pink-slipped every year over six straight years by two school systems. It's a sorry fate for a Phi Beta Kappa graduate from the best college in our state. Now he's making enough money part-time to go to grad school so he can become an administrator and change the system—or so he says. That's not very likely, I think, but I don't tell him that—who am I to kill obstinate optimism or to shatter the dreams of youth?

But that's another story—maybe even two stories. Anyway, we had been discussing schools for a while when Harvey Alkschmeer, an old friend of mine, sidles over a few seats and says, "Mind if I butt in?"—as he does so.

We don't mind, and he continues.

"I couldn't help hearing you guys talk about improving education with longer school years and all that. The real problem's *geography*. Nobody knows anything about geography any more—I was nuts about it when I was in school. Have you ever considered the Geographic Quotient?"

Geographic Quotient? Jake and I both draw blanks.

"Yeah. Take Japan, for instance. Measure its north-south distance, like maybe 1625 miles. Then divide that by its east-west distance, about 250 miles. You get a quotient of 6.5, and then you..."

What's that got to do with educational productivity, Harvey?

"Don't talk when I'm interrupting. Do the same for Sweden and you get a quotient of about 4.33. If you look at just the west half of Germany, it's a little less than two. For England, the GQ's about 1.25. Uh, you guys understand what quotients are, don't you?"

Of course we do. Both Jake and I teach math—when we're teaching.

"Well now, take the continental United States. Divide 1600 miles by 3000 miles and you get .53. There's the trouble; the quotient's too small. It's even worse if you include Hawaii and Alaska."

Wait a minute, Harvey. What's the difference if it's small?

"Take it easy—I'll get to that. Take the quotients for all those countries and run a correlation with the educational productivity figures you were talking about, just like you were doing when you were relating them to the length of school year. You'll find damn near a perfect correlation: the higher the GQ, the higher the productivity."

I know better than to break in again before he finishes.

"So the solution clearly is to change our quotient to bring it more in line with the countries with higher productivity, right?"

I venture a meek question, Just how would we do that?

"A couple of ways. We could add Canada and Mexico to the United States, and that would give us a Geographic Quotient of about 1.4. But that's not enough improvement, and it would make an awful lot of states, maybe 90—think of the stars in the flag! And then we'd have a bigger language problem, having to deal with both French and Spanish—on top of your southern lingo.

"So probably it would be better to divide the U.S. into four or five separate countries with new north-south boundaries—maybe call them Atlantis, Midland, Plains, Rockymont, and Westcoast. They'd have quotients of 2.0 to 3.2—not as good as Japan, but better than England or Germany. Think of what it would do to the productivity figures! Remember, we have to be competitive."

I glance at Jake and see his eyes roll. I know he's thinking the same as I: Harvey needs a big lesson in both statistics and political science, not to mention practicality.

"I can guess that you're skeptical, but look, the figures are right there, just like they are for the length of the school year. My theory's supported just as much as the other."

Harvey, that's a simple solution. Every complex problem has a simple solution, and it's usually wrong.

"Hey, I know who said that—some guy named Mention or Munching or something. I've heard it quoted somewhere."

Mencken is the name—H. L. Mencken, once with the Baltimore *Sun*.

"I might have known he was some crazy writer. But why isn't my simple solution as good as those other guys'?"

Maybe it is—maybe none of them are worth anything.

"Well, figures don't lie, you know."

Harvey, I give up; you're incorrigible and I've always thought it a waste of time and energy to try to corrugate the incorrigible.

"Hey, neat phrase. I'll have to remember that. Well, I'd better get going—see ya," he says as he drains his glass and gets up.

"But think carefully about longer school years and Geographic Quotients, won't you?"

Jake pours another soda for each of us. We just shake our heads as Harvey Alkschmeer disappears out the door.

Yeah, we'll think about them. And all those other simple one-dimensional solutions to educational problems. Very carefully.

16

More Lessons of the Open Road

The pursuit of dreams, experience as a foundation for education, and other ruminations while rolling down the interstate in an eighteen-wheeler...

Recently in this column, I wrote of my experience accompanying a tractor-trailer driver as she transported freight across the country [see "Truckin' and Teachin'," Chapter 13]. That odyssey covered 8000-some miles in 25 days and induced a number of interesting perceptions.

Some of my friends were amused at my description of the satisfactions and frustrations of truck driving. They thought trucking was much like teaching. And my description of working conditions in the trucking industry reminded them of conditions in some universities.

Indeed, I found that the work of trucking had parallels in the work of teaching. My open-road adventure brought some important aspects of teaching into sharper focus.

For example, teaching requires careful planning and the orchestration of many elements in order to reach the destination of student learning. It requires anticipation of the unexpected and constant adjustment to changing circumstances. It requires a calm equanimity in the face of frustration. It requires commitment and dedication, performing even its humble tasks as though they were great and noble.

But my intent here is not to rehash these lessons. Rather, I want to add two more to the list reported earlier.

First, my trip reinforced many of my thoughts about experience as a foundation for education. Meaning and value and learning can be drawn from any experience—even trucking, as unlikely as that might seem at first glance. But gaining these benefits from experience doesn't just happen, and it requires more than just openness of mind. It requires deliberate questioning and reflecting. We must always keep ourselves in these modes. And if we desire the same benefits for our students, we must generate these modes in them, too.

Further, we must never lose our willingness to seek out and undergo new experience, to walk in others' moccasins, to take the new road (even its detours) wherever it may lead us. To do otherwise is to run a risk of not learning, not growing, and ultimately not living.

The second lesson is more poignant. Before I embarked on my trucking adventure, I found a surprising number of people— both men and women—who said "I always wanted to drive a truck," or "I wish I could do what you are doing." (John Steinbeck encountered much of the same as he embarked on his travels with Charley, nearly 30 years prior to my journey.) It would be easy to dismiss these statements as the remnants of foolish dreams, but I think they reflect something much deeper. I find here more a residual of longing and of remorse over a road not taken.

My thoughts are drawn back to an article in *The Chronicle of Higher Education* (August 15, 1990, p. B2) by John R. Coleman, former professor, administrator, and college and foundation president, lately turned innkeeper in Chester, Vermont. Coleman says (and I paraphrase here) that the dreams that stir us to excited wakefulness at 2:30 a.m. are the ones to pursue, but they often succumb to suppression by our "sensible" self in the harsh morning light of safety and convention.

My daughter, the driver/guide on my trucking/learning adventure last fall, is a case in point. Though a crack typist at 120 WPM, she detested the conditions of office work. Yet it took her nearly a dozen years to break the bonds of convention before switching to a new career in the demanding world of trucking. At 115 pounds, she successfully wrestles a rig that weighs in at 40 tons when fully loaded, and she enjoys it. She has my admiration and support.

If I were to emphasize just one lesson from my trucking odyssey, it would be this: Have the courage to pursue dreams, despite the unknowns, despite the travails, despite the presumed "risks," despite the "logic" that says to play things safe and by the book—especially despite the confining conventions of society and the fear of what people might think. Many risks and constraints are ephemeral and will evaporate in the face of reality and determination.

Let me return to Coleman. He said that if he could leave only two bits of advice for his students, they would be these: We don't have to take the world as we find it, but we can work to change it for the better. Go where your heart and your head tell you to go.

From another quarter, John Keating in the film *Dead Poets Society* would add: Seize the day. Fight complacency. Don't let your life be ordinary.

Mighty good lessons all, I would say. Not just for our students but for all of us who teach them.

┌─ Response ────────────────────────────────────┐
│   │
│   │
│   │
│   │
│   │
│   │
│   │
│   │
│   │
│   │
│   │
└──┘

17

Milton's Well-Point Average

Simply add temperature, diastolic blood pressure, white cell count, and cholesterol level—then divide by four to get an index that's useful in a wide variety of interesting studies and medical decisions.

Ohmer Milton has long since retired from the University of Tennessee, where he was Professor of Psychology and Director of the Learning Research Center for many years, but he still stirs the educational pot frequently. And he is a devious rascal. He likes to plant ideas in someone's head, then walk away and let the person struggle with them.

So it was no surprise recently when he dropped me a note with his proposal for a well-point average. He gave me a few suggestions on how it might be used and then said, "See what you can do with it and send me a draft." That's what I mean: he's devious. And he knows where I'm most vulnerable. Ever since, my mind has been churning over the possibilities.

Milton calculates a well-point average—WPA—by adding a person's temperature, diastolic blood pressure, white cell count, and cholesterol level and then dividing by four. Although the measures are determined by different procedures, each is a simple number and one does not have to be an expert in order to interpret it. But by combining the four into a composite single figure one obtains an index that can be employed in a wide variety of interesting studies and medical decisions.

Milton observes that a *similar index* has served the halls of learning for nearly two centuries.

The well-point average could have many applications. For example, physicians could use it to determine the amount of medication to prescribe. It could be useful in connection with referrals to specialists. Nurses could use it to determine a number of things—whether to assign an extra nurse to a patient, how often to make bed checks at night, and length of stay for visitors, to mention just a few. Admitting personnel at a hospital could use the WPA to decide whether a patient rates a private room. It could be useful in deciding whether a patient should stay in the hospital or be discharged. Nursing homes could base judgments about skilled care on the WPA. And peer review boards in any health field would find it useful in matters of evaluation and certification.

All of this would have to be supported extensively by research, of course: studies relating the WPA to response to medication, overcoming infection, and the like. One could use the index to compare wellness from year to year in any cohort—not to mention between groups, among geographic regions, between the U.S. and Sweden, etc. Further, correlations could be made between the WPA and a myriad of other variables, such as drinking behavior, patterns of smoking, and stress level of occupations. It would be enough to generate dissertations for a decade or more, not to mention employment of research assistants, statisticians and computer experts, Milton suggests.

Colleges are sure to find many uses for the WPA, and the NCAA would likely incorporate it into eligibility requirements for athletic scholarships. Actuaries and other personnel in the life and health insurance trade would have a field day with the WPA. State agencies could use it in manipulating medical and welfare benefits. And can you imagine what would happen when Congress gets ahold of it?

On an individual basis, the WPA could be computed twice a year, say in December and May, to determine whether one's wellness is improving or declining. Physicians could post an honor roll of patients who do well on the WPA. Those who do poorly could be put on special diets. The WPA could be used to decide whether remedial exercise programs are indicated and then later to assess their effectiveness. Businesses, organizations and communities could stage friendly competitions based on the WPAs of their members. All of this requires that the WPA does not become inflated in certain venues, but that, again, is an appropriate matter for scientific investigation.

For individuals unable to obtain certain components of the WPA at a particular time (an unlikely situation, given the presence of various testing stations in shopping malls), a modified index could be constructed using temperature, pulse rate and breathing rate after climbing one flight of stairs. Even that could be useful in deciding whether to call your physician for a late-evening heartburn or to tough it out with nonprescription medications.

Once you start thinking about the WPA, its possibilities seem almost unlimited, particularly in our nation of healthy hypochondriacs.

So there you have it in essence: Milton's famous well-point average. What? You're skeptical? Oh, Ye of Little Statistical Faith! You say that figuring the WPA is like averaging apples and oranges? (Gee—they're both fruit; what's wrong with fruit salad?) You think the WPA's applications are overdrawn beyond all reason?

Well, if you know Ohmer Milton, you know he's a master at evaluation. And for years he's been a critic of its excesses, such as contrived indices, flawed statistics, over-reliance on correlations, minute discriminations taken to the third decimal place, and inappropriate applications. (He sometimes describes himself as a cynical psychologist.) If you know Ohmer, you'd suspect that ol' rascal of pulling our legs just a bit in order to make an obtuse point or two about a certain well-known index in Academe, one that we use for all sorts of minor and major decisions.

And, you know, we might well take his points to heart. Often it gets even more ridiculous than the hypothetical uses of the proposed WPA. Students' academic careers and even their lives sometimes hang in the balance of a few hundredths of a point. And inconsistencies? I know of one institution that will elect students to the nation's most prestigious scholastic honorary at the junior level with a 3.650, whereas at another campus only 30 miles away graduating seniors with a 3.650 will be rejected.

Some will argue that the grade-point average is necessary in order to make academic discriminations about retention, honors, admission to graduate study, and the like. Some will ask, "What index will take its place?"

Milton's answer is direct: "Nothing. It is just plain wrong to make decisions about a student on the basis of a number. Evaluating a person—and students certainly are persons—requires judgment. Don't duck the responsibility."

Ohmer Milton once again is spurring us to take a long, hard look at our habitual and often arbitrary practices in educational evaluation and grading—and all to the good. Isn't it time to consider real factors and real individuals and their real lives rather than statistical designations?

Response

18

Seven Principles of Teaching Seldom Taught in Grad School

Some of the most practical teaching principles are acquired through experience.

In Olden Days, beginning teachers typically were given a book, a list of chapters to cover, and a class roster. That was the totality of our preparation. We reported to the assigned room at the assigned time and started teaching. Remarkably, most of us somehow survived.

My first classroom stint, as a teaching fellow back in those halcyon Wisconsin days, carried an annual payment of $940 for teaching three semester-long courses; I also got a break on tuition for my graduate studies. I felt so privileged that I splurged seven dollars a week on a luxury room in a professor's home.

Not just stipends have changed over the years. Today's teaching assistants receive extensive orientations and sometimes even take courses to prepare for the classroom. Certainly, it's all for the better.

But for all the improvement, the professoriate of the future seldom encounters in grad school some of the more practical principles of teaching which are acquired through experience. Each veteran who has toiled for years in the knowledge industry has a personal collection. Here are seven time-tested principles from mine.

1. You don't have to know all the answers.

Of course, one can *never* know all the answers, but neophyte teachers often think they have to exhibit omniscience. All teachers need to develop comfortable strategies for dealing with questions that temporarily stump them. Admitting you don't know the answer is a good and honest start; but pledge that you will search for one. Sometimes answers arrive more easily once you clear distracting thoughts from your mind. (Remember this when a question you present to students temporarily stumps them.)

And you don't have to answer every question the moment it's asked. Some questions require more time than is available at the end of a class hour—a good reason for programming the question period about two-thirds the way through a class, rather than at the end. In other instances, it can be instructive for students to observe you—and assist you—as you work through the process of finding an answer. Consider also guiding question askers to their *own* answers.

2. One of the best things that can happen to you is losing your notes from the last time you taught the course.

We all like to build on our experience and improve each time we teach a course again. But sometimes our notes from a previous run can be only a crutch. If you lose those notes (or deliberately put them aside) you are more likely to rethink the teaching-learning process, develop new perspectives, and introduce creative innovations.

3. It's more important to determine how much you dare leave out of a class session than to figure out how to jam everything in.

It's always a temptation to teach everything you know. But it's better to select just the right content and program it in just the right way. Furthermore, it's important to determine what to leave out of "instruction" so that students can gain the benefit (and sometimes even joy) of discovering things and learning on their own.

4. One answer can be given to almost every educational question: "It all depends..."

Theory, research, anticipation, and preparation all are useful when educational decisions have to be made. But every situation is unique. In the final analysis, what one decides, what one does at any particular moment is a judgement call. That call depends on a multitude of variables, many of which cannot be foreseen, much less fore-judged. A teacher has to select whatever option seems to lead to the greatest learning benefit.

5. Cartoon characters can often express things more effectively than faculty members.

There are several factors that seem to make cartoon characters more memorable than mere human professors: humor, familiarity, identification, and—above all—the essence of a lesson compressed into just a few images. For evidence, I submit the example below. But use cartoons appropriately and sparingly, as you would any dramatic flourish. And be sure to secure permission from the copyright holder before you use a cartoon.

6. It's OK to have a bad day occasionally. Just never have two in a row.

Few of us can score a 10 every day in the classroom. And all of us can hit a really down day, perhaps through no fault of our own. Accept it and ensure that the next meeting of the class is so good that it more than makes up for the temporary lapse.

7. Don't take things—especially yourself— so damn seriously.

We all need to be reminded of the value of breaking intense activity with relaxation, modifying one-track dedication with varied experience, and enhancing well-being with humor. The flowers in life are not just for botanophils; take time to stop and smell a few yourself. But remember that lightening up is not an excuse for slacking off or treating teaching casually.

My selection may not be the most important seven principles of teaching, but I think they can serve teachers well, even if they're seldom taught in grad school. I'm happy to share them with you. And I welcome your sharing with me other useful principles that you've discovered through your own experience.

┌─ Response ──────────────────────────────────┐
│   │
│   │
│   │
│   │
│   │
│   │
│   │
│   │
│   │
│   │
│   │
│   │
└───┘

19

Mozart, Big Rigs, *Alabama*, and Teaching

What connections are possible among vastly different worlds?

I've just been through an unusual week.

It started on Sunday with a performance of Mozart's monumental *Requiem,* in which I participated as a member of the 120-voice chorus. It ended yesterday with a visit to the 21st Annual Mid-America Trucking Show in Louisville, capped off with attending a performance by the country group *Alabama.*

I sit here on Saturday morning with the remnants of fugues mixing in my head with the sounds of "Born Country," pondering my experiences in these vastly different worlds.

And a backdrop for all this is a comment made by a friend recently, characterizing me as "having an ability to make connections." This morning, I think I'm facing my greatest challenge in that regard.

Should I compare and contrast the reactions of the audiences of the two concerts? A complex and difficult task that would be. Suffice it to say, the Mozart audience didn't sing the *Requiem* along with us. They didn't flick butane lighters and hold them aloft during the "Lacrimosa" and other especially moving passages. And they didn't scream during our singing of the "Dies Irae," as appropriate as that might have been to enhance our musical portrayal of the days of wrath.

Should I speculate on how many people, professional or general public, might show up at an educational expo, compared to a truck show? That would probably lead to the obvious: the crowds drawn to education (and Mozart) are minuscule, compared to the many thousands drawn to big rigs (and *Alabama).*

Should I analyze the techniques of *Alabama* in firing up an audience, seeking to discover how they might apply in the classroom? Should I examine what elements produce such a moving experience, even for me? No way. (But I confess that during the *Alabama* concert, my mind frequently drifted to that consideration.)

So what am I left with? What connections are possible?

People are people, but they vary widely. There are many worlds outside the academic world. Many of our students live also in other worlds. It will help us to teach them if we know something about their frames of reference.

Our recognizing the many diverse worlds around us does not require our evaluating one against the other. Each world can be appropriate and valid for those within it.

We need not fight these other worlds. Neither do we need to join or give in to them, emulating their approaches and appeals.

A better alternative is to learn how to be ourselves in our own world. And let us value the benefits brought by the diversity of other worlds.

Whether performing classical music or country music, whether teaching or trucking, people achieve excellence in their own ways. Let us learn how to be excellent, no matter what our fields or our endeavors.

Surely there is value to crossover experiences such as I've just had. They enrich us. They help expand our world and provide us broadened perspective. They help us appreciate our own world. And they help condition us for new experiential contrasts. (I'm already anticipating the excitement of another unusual week I'll spend later this month, visiting writers, quiltmakers, basketmakers and other friends in Blackey, Caney Creek, Wolfpen, and similar remote places in eastern Kentucky—with all of this bracketed on one end with an NCAA regional basketball final game and on the other with hiking in the Red River Gorge.)

In the final analysis, probably each thing *is* connected to every other thing—as John Muir and many others have said—though we may not always readily perceive the interrelations.

Let us savor and rejoice in each experience of life as it comes, no matter when or where that is.

But I still fantasize a bit about what might happen to my ratings as a teacher if I had the effects of a computer-driven bank of 200 lights enhancing my classroom performance, not to mention an enthralled bunch of groupies sitting (standing? dancing?) in the front row, infecting the rest of my students with their enthusiastic response. And I wonder what it would be like just once to have someone raise a flaming lighter overhead when I made a neat point in class.

The methods by which teachers can generate response and engagement in students vary perhaps as much as the different worlds vary. Since most students (as well as teachers) live within several worlds, the interconnectedness may indicate multiple approaches in reaching students.

Each of us must discover what will capture the involvement of each student, no matter what are that student's worlds. Our success in doing that will be reflected in students' learning—and in our personal satisfaction, as well.

Response

20

Students Become Data— Statistics Comes Alive

Every teacher longs for ways to convince students early on that course material is useful, interesting, and capable of being mastered. Here's a strategy for doing this in introductory statistics.

Every teacher longs for ways to convince students early on that course material is useful, interesting, and capable of being mastered. I've found a neat strategy for doing this in introductory statistics, as unlikely as that may seem to those who have struggled with the subject.

On the first day of class, I ask for six to eight volunteers— not sensitive about their height, weight, or grade-point average—to come forward and arrange themselves in a line according to height. Other students verify that the arrangement is reasonably accurate. I give each volunteer a blue card with a number to designate rank in height.

Then I ask the volunteers to confer and to rearrange themselves by weight. They do, and I pass out green cards to designate rank in weight. I ask the observers whether they think there is a relationship between height and weight.

"Well, some…," they might say.

"How strong?" I press. They hesitate. We recognize the need to quantify our statements.

That's when I pull out the short-cut formula for Spearman's rank-order correlation coefficient. I ask each volunteer to find the difference between the blue and green numbers and square it, producing a d^2 for each. As I add these squared differences, I introduce the concept of summation and its symbol, $\sum$. We plug the sum and the value of n (the number of volunteers) into the formula

$$r_s = 1 - \frac{6 \sum d_i^2}{n(n^2 - 1)}$$

and calculate the correlation coefficient, r_s. Perhaps it's between +.60 and +.75, depending on the mix of sexes. We observe that if the relationship were "perfect," each difference would be zero and thus $\sum d_i^2$ would be zero, producing a coefficient of +1.00.

Can we expect height and weight to be related similarly in the general population? I project a simple table onto a screen and ask the students to accept it on faith (something to get used to early in statistics). We note that +.60 might not be statistically significant unless we have more data—say, over eight pairs of values.

Then I ask the volunteers to arrange themselves according to grade-point average. They do, amidst lots of chuckling. The observers suggest that the relationship between GPA and height (or weight) is weak or perhaps "sort of turned around a little." I distribute red cards and we calculate two new coefficients: GPA-height, GPA-weight. They might be in the vicinity of –.35. We talk about negative correlations and determine that the coefficient for a "perfect" negative correlation would be –1.00.

Could one eat more and grow into a taller basketball player? Eat less and improve one's GPA? Students laugh and quickly distinguish between correlation between two variables and cause-and-effect.

Thus, in fifteen to twenty minutes, a number of statistical concepts are introduced and worked with. Students are doing statistics; they find that it's not too hard. Never mind that correlation doesn't come up until the end of the course, that students don't yet know how to compute standard deviations, or that they can't distinguish among mean, mode, and median. They are turned on, learning easily, and enjoying it. Best of all, students are actively involved in the subject. It's a great start for the course.

Response

21

Seven Qualities of Highly Effective Teachers

By themselves, these seven qualities may not be sufficient criteria for teaching excellence—but they may be pretty close to essential conditions.

The number *seven* seems to have magical properties that attract people to it.

The universe was created in seven days, according to *Genesis*, and we now have seven days in a week. There are seven theological and cardinal virtues (faith, hope, charity, prudence, justice, fortitude, temperance). Likewise, there are seven deadly sins (pride, covetousness, lust, anger, gluttony, envy, sloth). The liberal arts of the middle ages numbered seven, chunked into a quadrivium (arithmetic, geometry, astronomy, music) and a trivium (grammar, rhetoric, logic). And today, fortunate faculty members may be granted sabbatical leaves.

On a more mundane plane, seven is the most probable sum when rolling two dice. Seven digits (such as a telephone number) are generally all that most people can store in short-term memory. And if you want your slide or overhead projector transparency to be readable, don't put more than seven lines on it, with each line no longer than seven words.

So it's not unexpected that an American Association for Higher Education commission focused on "Seven Principles of Good Practice in Undergraduate Education," and Steven Covey wrote a best seller *Seven Habits of Highly Effective People.* I even read a recent journal article by an off-beat writer: "Seven

Principles of Teaching Seldom Taught in Grad School" [see Chapter 18].

Seven is not quite in the same number league with the *three* of Liberté-égalité-fraternité, but it's a good cut or two above the *ten* of David Letterman's lists. Propelled by this mystical momentum of the number, I give below my nominations for qualities of highly effective teachers—seven in number, of course.

1. Highly effective teachers *care*. They care about their students, their work, and themselves. They treat others with dignity; they respect others' integrity. They give high priority to benefitting others. They affirm others' strengths and beings; it's a kind of love.

2. Highly effective teachers *share*. They share their knowledge, insights, and viewpoints with others. Their willingness to share is a way of life for them. They don't withhold information for personal gain.

3. Highly effective teachers *learn*. They continually seek truth and meaning. They seek to discover new ideas and insights. They reflect on their experiences and incorporate the learning therefrom into their lives. They are willing to upgrade their skills. They continue growing and developing throughout their lives.

4. Highly effective teachers *create*. They are willing to try the new and untested, to take risks for worthy educational outcomes. Anything worth doing is worth failing at. They are not discouraged by an occasional failure; they reframe the error as an opportunity to do better as a result of the experience.

5. Highly effective teachers *believe*. They have faith in students. They trust students and are willing to grant them freedom and responsibility. They hold high expectations for their students, as well as for themselves.

6. Highly effective teachers *dream*. They have a vision of success. They are driven by an image of excellence, the best that their innate abilities allow. They always seek to im-

prove, never being content with just "getting by" in teaching or in any other endeavor.

7. Highly effective teachers *enjoy*. Teaching is not just employment to them; it is their Work. They throw themselves into it with vigor. They gain major satisfaction and joy from it. And that joy often infects their students.

While this particular set of qualities is my own compilation, I've found in workshops where we've examined what is meant by "good teaching" that these qualities are prominently mentioned. By themselves they may not be sufficient conditions for teaching excellence, but they may be pretty close to essential.

Surely, you say, there are other qualities that should make the list. What about critical thinking, positive attitude, or calm equanimity, for example? What about patience? Well, certainly a case could be made for all of these—and others, I'm sure.

But eleven (though the next prime number after seven) is not such a magical number. And keeping practicality in mind, it's harder for one to retain more than seven in memory.

So if you can keep in mind *care, share, learn, create, believe, dream,* and *enjoy,* you may keep them actively in practice. And that will move you toward becoming a highly effective teacher.

22

Thinking Otherwise

---

*It is entirely reasonable and appropriate for
teachers to question whether our beliefs are
consistent with the present state of knowledge of
human behavior and whether these beliefs serve the
growth and development of others.*

A timeworn definition of a professor is "someone who thinks
otherwise."

In my experience, that statement is somewhat short on
evidence (and really not very long on humor, either). So it's
always been a delight when a few people emerge out of the mass
of conventionality and do "think otherwise." They've been my
best teachers and my most helpful colleagues.

That delight was renewed recently when I attended a conference with Allen Menlo, a friend from 'way back in my dear
old Ann Arbor days (to quote from a venerable Michigan song).
Al is Professor Emeritus of Education at Michigan but still
actively engaged in several international education projects.

Among other collaborations in the past, Al and I were part
of a three-person team who conducted a college teaching course
in Extension. Although we would have discussed our game plan
throughout the week prior to each class, on Thursday evening
when we piled into the car to drive to Orchard Lake, invariably
Al would ask, "Now what is it we want to do tonight?" For the
next 40 miles, we rehashed and often changed our strategy for
the class. Furthermore, these on-the-road planning sessions
always put us into just the right character and frame of mind
to enter the classroom at the end of the run.

I learned from Al that no plan should be set in concrete—there is always room for spontaneity and new perspectives. I learned to be comfortable with a considerable degree of uncertainty in the classroom. Prepare, yes; but let instruction be a live, creative activity that unfolds before the students. These lessons served me well for many years.

That's why it was such an enjoyable experience to spend four days with Al this past June. At the Wakonse Conference, Al conducted a session based on the premise that our personal beliefs shape our teaching behavior. Accepting that, then it would be useful for each of us to occasionally reexamine our beliefs and ask whether they are consistent with the present state of knowledge about human behavior. Further, we should consider how our beliefs about people best serve their growth and development. It seems an entirely reasonable and appropriate activity for teachers to engage in.

Al posed what he thought were several beliefs that people commonly held. An exercise among the workshop participants (teachers from several universities) generally verified this. Then Al presented alternate viewpoints contrary to these beliefs, with considerable supporting evidence from research and literature. It was a provocative seminar that made us think about our own behavior and possible adjustments therein. It was a prime example of a teacher's thinking otherwise that generated learning. And it was Al Menlo at his finest.

What follows deals with three of the beliefs. It is largely quoted and paraphrased from Al's session, our subsequent conversations, and his draft of a paper on the topic.

Belief: Clarity and specificity of objectives in learning is more a good thing than a bad thing.

Alternate viewpoint: Defining specifically the final results of educational efforts strongly precludes ending up at a place one could never have imagined at the beginning of the venture, thereby reducing the opportunity for honest, open inquiry into the future. The best state of improvement is not known until arriving there, and the experience of moving toward it holds greater potential for discovering that truly best state than anticipating it.

The promotion of richest growth occurs when one develops a general idea or image of a goal, aspiration, or hoped-for outcome, and then searchingly and openly makes efforts toward this *goalward imagery*. It is the sense of *directionality*, coupled with inertial guidance, that moves a person toward an as-yet-to-be-determined specific outcome. Though the outcome probably changes as one moves closer to it, each change is likely to bring an increase in the clarity of the developing outcome, as well as the emergent paths toward it.

Belief: Evaluation of performance, while sometimes a disliked responsibility, can be an importantly useful service of one person to another.

Alternate viewpoint: Evaluation and judgment damage the health and trustfulness of an interpersonal relationship, as well as reduce either party's receptiveness to being influenced by the other. What *can* be helpful to the growth and development of either person are feedback processes which involve the non-evaluative observation of behavior, the non-judgmental citing of consequences, and the inquiry of whether the consequences are in line with the intent of the behavior.

Feedback should be comprised of neutral information, untainted by evaluation; it is inappropriate to speak of "positive feedback" and "negative feedback." Criticism leads to arousal of resistance, occurrence of losses of esteem, and deterioration of possibilities for mutual helpfulness. Under many circumstances, praise can produce undesirable affect, particularly when praise is insincere, undeserved, or inconsistent with the self-knowledge of the person being praised. Even when praise alone is employed, praise not extended can easily be interpreted as masked or unstated criticism.

Belief: Most persons resist change more than they seek change.

Alternate viewpoint: All living things have an inherent drive for change—an activeness, curiosity, and search for betterment. What persons do resist are expected *consequences* of change which might diminish their self or social esteem or involve their possible loss of power, perquisites, comfort, and material belongings. When such expectations arise, the natural drive for change is halted as energy is directed into resisting the expected loss.

It is not until the person can reduce the expectation of loss, gain control of the loss process, or reframe expected loss into a non-loss or a tolerable loss, that resistance will be dissipated or eliminated. Then persons are free to exercise their natural strivings for action and change.

A teacher who embraces the three alternate viewpoints above would display teaching behaviors significantly different from what is customary or currently advocated.

Instead of rigorously identifying specific behavioral outcomes, a teacher would focus more on helping individuals develop and clarify their general images of desired personal changes. The teacher would help learners seek and remain receptive to learning opportunities within the boundaries of their established directionality.

Instead of concentrating on elaborate, comprehensive, and cheat-proof evaluation mechanisms and grading schemes (the commonly-cited bane of teaching and a frequent source of ethical problems), a teacher would focus more on providing non-judgmental feedback on whether the outcomes of students' behavior are consistent with their intentions.

Instead of trying to force change on students through lock-step classroom and curricular demands, a teacher would focus more on helping students clarify the outcomes of educational growth and change. A teacher would also help students cope with the expectation of loss, whether real or imagined, in order to restore energy to the drive for action and change in response to stimulation from self or from others.

Behaviors such as these could clearly affect the character of teaching and learning as we now know it. Learners would be engaged more integrally in a process of actualizing their potentials, guided by their sense of directionality. Teachers would be engaged more integrally in aiding students' growth endeavors. Though teachers might not be able to play such a role exclusively, given today's large enrollments, this stance would serve well when appropriate opportunities arise, even if for only a few students.

Whether or not you agree with the proposed alternate viewpoints, whether or not you accept their implications for teaching, I hope you've been stimulated and challenged by Al Menlo's thinking otherwise. Perhaps you may have become more aware of your own sense of directionality. Perhaps you may view your work and your students differently. Perhaps you have grown just a bit. And perhaps you, too, may question a few "accepted beliefs" and begin to think otherwise about some things.

Response

23

Second Thoughts on Timeworn Clichés

The verbal shorthand of clichés often does us disservice. Good teaching requires the imaginative integration of many particulars, not the application of simplistic formulas.

Like many teachers, I'm an inveterate clipper of articles and collector of materials that I think will be useful some day in some way. Unlike the sensible accumulators, I just don't seem to have time to develop a system for filing and retrieving these would-be gems.

I've been at this activity so long that the stacks in my study have overflowed into the hallway and partway down the stairs, much to the consternation of my family. Every once in a while I remember an item that I'd like to use, and a prolonged search begins. Whether or not I find what I'm looking for, I usually encounter quite a few things that I had forgotten about, and I pull them out for further consideration. (Because I don't have time to deal with them all, some wind up on yet a *new* stack!)

The other day I was engaged in such a search when I serendipitously rediscovered a thought-provoking article by Bobby Fong, "Commonplaces about Teaching: Second Thoughts" (*Change*, July/August 1987, pp. 28-34). In it, Fong expresses discomfort with six commonplaces that seem to be "verbal shorthand meant to call reflexive agreement."

Consider, for example, *The silent student is an uninvolved learner.* Fong argues that this presumption neglects to examine *why* students might be silent and whether they are *really* uninvolved. Silence may not be a sign of apathy; it may not indicate an inability or unwillingness to participate. Silence can be *active*—the learner may be keeping up with what is said, processing it, and anticipating what is to come. Good listening requires silence. And silence may be culturally related—for example, it may be a sign of respect. Rather than simply calling on silent students to speak, as so many of us do, we might better encourage them to see speaking as another avenue to learning, help them develop skills of discussion, and help them find their own voices. (In this paragraph, I've paraphrased from the article).

Similarly, Fong questions and qualifies five additional commonplaces:

- *Grades are a necessary evil.*

- *Discussion is preferable to lecture.*

- *Teachers are fellow-learners with their students.*

- *Students need to acquire skills, not memorize information.*

- *Instruction must be geared to student backgrounds and aspirations.*

Fong argues that it is difficult for any maxim to encompass teaching in all its diversity. "Teachers must moderate the dictates of laudable but divergent general principles in pursuit of an imaginative integration involving a thousand particulars of culture, student, and instructor. Teaching is thus idiosyncratic, resistant to generalization." His second thoughts are to be considered seriously, and I commend the article to all teachers.

Well, the Fong article turned my mind to some of the clichés which commonly arise in teaching and to which we often give reflexive agreement. It seems to me that they, too, should be given second thoughts, questioned and qualified as Fong does his commonplaces.

We've all heard this one: *If it ain't broke, don't fix it.* The intended message seems to be, If something seems to be running smoothly, tinkering with it may bollix it up. But often there is a hidden message: Let things alone; there are no complaints; don't change. When we stop to think of it, there is often good reason to discover potential breakdowns and preclude their occurring, rather than making repairs only after malfunction, with attendant loss of service or injury to person. (Consider, for example, aircraft preventive maintenance programs.)

In teaching, no course is without the potential for improvement. By continually making small changes for the better ("tinkering"), that improvement is gradual and constant. It avoids the stagnancy that can taint repeated runs of a course. Too, by monitoring the consequences and outcomes of teaching efforts—and adjusting appropriately—dysfunction might be precluded.

Don't reinvent the wheel presumes to prevent wasting energy on something that has already been done. But none of us or our students were present when the wheel or other significant innovations were invented, and we've been denied the joys of such discovery, not to mention the instructive benefit of the process. So perhaps some "wheels" might well be "reinvented" continually.

Furthermore, there are many kinds of wheels, and repeating the process of responding to a need may produce a wheel (or perhaps even an entirely new product) that is more functional. I think of this particularly with regard to courses that we've taught before. We could simply (and "efficiently") repeat the process and plan that we've done previously, but better results are likely to result if we start anew and rethink how to accomplish our goals more effectively.

No pain, no gain fails my test of worthiness for several reasons. Though gain *can* result from painful situations, many benefits accrue to people without pain. One person's "pain" may be another's "exhilaration." Difficulty in surmounting obstacles and meeting challenges is not synonymous with pain.

The teacher who succumbs to this outworn cliché mistakenly thinks that pain must be inflicted on students for learning to occur and deliberately concocts painful experiences and justifies them in the name of learning. That's far, far from what we should be doing in teaching.

Start out tough; you can always ease up later (known in some circles as "Don't smile 'til Christmas") presumes that it's easier to go from toughness to sweetness than vice versa. Even if that might be true, why is being "tough" important at all? One can hold high expectations for students without being "tough." One can still demand excellence from them without being unpleasant.

Furthermore, whatever pattern a teacher establishes at the beginning of a course is likely to prevail thereafter. Attempts to change may not only be difficult but may also send confusing signals to students. Better to start in the appropriate pattern and maintain as much consistency as possible. And don't confuse consistency with rigidity; retain some flexibility to make changes in-course.

We may not think of this next phrase as a cliché, but we resort to it so commonly (I myself have done so twice already in this article) that it certainly should qualify: *I just don't have time for [whatever]*. True, most of us have more on our plate than we can consume. But when we cover inaction or failure to accept an assignment by defaulting to the time excuse, we often are being simply evasive. We all have had the experience of having something arise suddenly and unexpectedly to which we respond immediately. When we say that we don't have time for something, we often mean that we choose to not assign it high priority, given other things that are competing for our attention. Why not be entirely honest and speak in terms of priority instead of time?

Two American pop philosophers are responsible for my final outworn cliché. Julius Marx is credited with *It's not over until the fat lady sings*, and Lawrence Peter Berra is reported to have coined the alternate form: *It's not over until it's over*. (Yogi, however, is big on denial: "I never said a lot of the things I said.") We could support extinguishing Groucho's version quite quickly because of its sexism and weightism. But the essence of both phrases is still: There's *always* hope (for success, winning, passing the course, whatever) even until the bitter end.

As one who sometimes closes letters with "Esperance," I recognize that situations have a greater possibility for a desirable outcome than we may realize, and success may result from hard work and persistence. So one should be cautious about premature resignation to less than we wish for.

But there are *some* situations in which maintaining hope against high odds is both unrealistic and undesirable. Better to cut our losses, salvage what we can, and redirect our energies to those things that have more reasonable possibilities for accomplishment. For example, a student might sometimes be better off to admit defeat in one course in order to concentrate on others which hold greater hope, rather than risk sinking in all courses. In a different setting, there are occasions in meetings when further debate serves little purpose if the outcome of an issue is clearly inevitable.

I hope this article by now has caused you to think of other clichés employed in teaching that have questionable value. I'm sure there are many to be relegated to the trash can of Academe. Such phrases are born with elements of truth. They grow through some basic utility. They become popular through repetition. Some become cutesy and end up on posters listing the endless variations of Murphy's Law. Then they become entrenched catch phrases and verbal shorthand that appeal to our reflexes. And some do us great disservice.

Teaching is complex and requires much more than simplistic formulas. We must question the outworn clichés and, as Bobby Fong says, pursue an imaginative integration of the thousand (or more) particulars that affect our teaching. That pursuit *will* serve us well.

┌─ Response ───

│
│
│
│
│
│
│
│
│
│
│
│
│
└──

24

Confessions of a Closet Thespian

Lessons learned from life upon the wicked stage can enhance teaching effectiveness even if you're not quite ready for prime time.

Mine was a classic case. All the telltale signs. Denial. Then guilt. Years of hiding it even from my friends. Finally, relief as I came out into the open: I was a Thespian at heart.

Like most adult behavior, it began many years ago in the tender days of my youth. I recall the grade school assembly one February when I delivered my very first lines on stage ("Four score and seven years ago..."). I had always thought I had done it because of parental pressure. My first role in high school was an expressman who delivered a crate of penguins to The Man Who Came to Dinner ("They got Coca-Cola this morning and liked it"). I did it just to be sociable with my theatrical friends, I thought. My first lead came in college in a one-act play ("The valiant never taste of death but once"). I thought I got the role because the campus was depleted of men by the armed forces. I should have known then, but I didn't.

On it went. Performing in choral groups. Writing scripts for short films. For years. Then slowly but surely it dawned. It was writ all over me, in not one letter large and scarlet, but three: HAM.

I enjoyed being front-and-center. I enjoyed commanding the attention of an audience. I enjoyed engaging them in my material. It gave me kicks.

But that is not my deepest confession. Those are not my sins most grave. Far more serious is that in teaching, my vocation—what I did for money, as well as for love—I applied so poorly all the things I had learned, and learned so well avocationally. For teaching is a performing art, as surely as is singing, dancing, and acting (and preaching, some would say). It requires capturing the interest and attention of students, and it requires stimulating their emotions and response in order to engage them in the material.

And I was doing that so poorly. What were my entrances like? Stimulating? Brisk? Communicating the character of what was to come? Not at all. Typically, I sauntered into the room, sat on the edge of my desk, studied my watch, glanced around, and when the house was reasonably full I brought my students to intense concentration with these pearls of the wisdom that was to follow: "Well, not everyone's here yet, but I guess we better get started."

My alternate entrance (I seemed to have only two) was even worse. I'd confer with students, conduct office activity, and take phone calls right up to class time. Then I'd grab my books and dash to the classroom—and spend the next several minutes catching my breath and warming up on the students. Would an actor ever subject an audience to that?

And my exits? I'm almost afraid to tell you. At the end of the hour I might wait as long as I could before the rustling of coats and the shuffling of feet forced me to say something like this: "Well, I wanted to squeeze Alkschmeer's Formula in today, but I guess there's not time. We'll have to save it for tomorrow—but let me give you just a brief look at it... " By the time I made my last gasp, many students had packed their books and gone on to their next classes. What actor or playwright could survive such an uninspiring finale?

How did I use my "dramatic arena" in the classroom? I confess that I confined my movements to the shallow triangle defined by the ends of the chalkboard and the center-positioned desk. No sweeping moves toward the wings, no movement down the aisles to engage students individually and intimately. And I didn't energize the audience and reabsorb some of that energy to enhance my work. Sad to say, at times I even walked on students' lines.

There were more sins of both commission and omission, but I need not dwell further on my dismal fall from grace.

Eventually it became clear to me that there are many similarities between the classroom and the performing hall. Many of the things that performers do to capture attention, engage the audience, and stimulate response can be done by teachers. Furthermore, many of these behaviors are already within teachers' repertoires or can be developed easily.

Over the past several years, I've collected and tried to state succinctly a number of such behaviors. For example, here are three clusters of suggestions for teachers to consider in preparing and initiating instruction:

- Warm up, both physically and mentally, before entering class, if only for a few minutes. Set your mood and manner. Get into character for the particular class and material. Rehearse your activity with a rapid mental run-through.

- Develop a variety of positive, active entrances and choose one for a particular class that best fits the situation.

- Select simple, but appropriate props to illustrate and punctuate classroom presentations and activities. A single item of attire often can create an entire character.

Performers—teachers included—are communicators. Of course, they communicate verbally. Many nonverbal behaviors also come into play. Thus, these suggestions for appropriate behaviors in the classroom setting:

- Develop a repertoire of gestures, movements, poses, and dramatic pauses and use them to highlight and emphasize material.

- Position yourself in the room according to the effects you want to achieve. Move toward students when you want to engage them more.

- Show emotion with your voice and body, particularly with expression on your face and in your eyes. Make eye contact with many students.

Teaching, like acting, is a dynamic activity that constantly depends on, and plays against the reactions and response of the audience. Therefore:

- Never do anything the same way for very long. Modulate your voice, change your mood, adjust the dynamics, and mix styles of instruction in order to provide emphasis and variety.

- Tune in to the response of your students and modify your teaching accordingly. Respond spontaneously. Try to create moments of surprise and of the unexpected during teaching.

Exits are important for teachers because they can send students away highly charged and eager to engage the material further. Don't let closings be generated only by the end of the hour or students' shutting down. Rather:

- Deliver your closing lines and make your exit on your own terms. Try to end a few moments early, while you still have attention.

It is not just the actor who carries the show. The theatrical design of the production is critical to a successful outcome. So, too, is the design of classroom productions. Each course is an extended play unto itself. Each class meeting is a series of scenes, a unique entity that merits individual attention. These general suggestions can help teachers make the most of the finite stage time available to them:

- Lay out events as in a story. Plan relatively short segments to match students' experience and attention span; arrange them strategically. Build suspense. Give glimpses of things to come and clues to eventual outcomes.

- Vary techniques and pace. Don't overuse any one strategy. Provide contrasts, contradictions, shifts of perspective, and novel ideas. Save your most dramatic moves for the really important things.

- Design a flexible plan for each class to allow for improvisation, amplification, and adjustment to immediate circumstances. Timing—making an appropriate move at the right moment—is crucial.

- Economize on content. Delete distracting and extraneous material. Provide opportunity for students to contribute ideas and viewpoints.

We've all known teachers who merely delivered educational monologues; some occasionally added a joke or two to relieve the boredom. But teaching can be so much more than that. Teaching can be alive! Each of us has many options for activity to include in our instructional productions:

- Consider including short skits, live or taped, to trigger response. Portray particular positions; debate various sides of issues.

- Search for activities such as debates, caucuses, and role-playing that will allow and encourage students themselves to get into the act.

- Set the stage before class. Place things on the board or on the desk that will interest and intrigue students when they enter.

- Open with a segment that captures and focuses student attention and sets the tone and pattern for the remainder of the class period.

- Close with a segment that produces the condition you want students to be in. It need not always be a complete resolution of problems and issues raised. There can be benefit to ending on an open note that allows students to carry the experience away with them and continue working on it.

But let me be clear: good instruction does not have to be bells and whistles. We do not have to be entertainers or comedians, take on false characters, or pander to students in order to be effective teachers. Surely all of us can teach better than we now do. We can still be ourselves and incorporate new means of communication into our classroom activity to enhance our effectiveness. The occasional dramatic element can add special life and spice to our teaching (but use it as a spice—sparingly). Students are responsive to good teaching and will give support to our efforts. Best of all, we will gain greater satisfaction—and perhaps even joy—from our work.

Most of the suggestions contained herein are relatively easy to carry out. Choose a few that seem comfortable to you and try them; select more as you are able. Consider studying a videotape of your teaching and identifying aspects of your voice and movement style that you can improve. Develop a plan for strategic teaching: work toward developing the persona that best portrays the teaching role you wish to play and which capitalizes on your personal strengths.

Popular wisdom has it that one has to be at least a little bit crazy to go into teaching. Whether or not there is a grain of truth in that, why not make the most of your own individuality? Use all of your special resources. You, too, can survive in teaching without actually becoming totally sane. And both you and your students will enjoy it and benefit from it.

I like to think that there's a unique star within each of us—the teacher that we really can be—just waiting to shine out. And within each student, too, there is a star that can shine on its own—perhaps needing only a little encouragement from a teacher.

Response

25

What Louis Szathmáry Might Say about College Teaching

A master chef who is willing to share the secrets that "make" his recipes would probably have a few tips for success in the classroom.

I've never met Louis Szathmáry, but we've talked by telephone and I've always had a special feeling for him. For one thing, he and my father (though separated by a generation or two) are *honfitársak*—compatriots—sharing the same Transylvanian hometown back in the old country, Hungary. For another, Louis and I both enjoy the creativity of cooking, even though he is an expert and I am a mere amateur.

Indeed, Louis Szathmáry is a scholar of cooking. His extensive collection of cookbooks going back to the 14th century is now a rare research resource at the University of Iowa. Chef Louis performed his art at The Bakery, a top-rated Chicago restaurant for nearly 30 years. Alas, it closed a few years back—before I could experience all of its continental classics.

But Louis's recipes live on in the several cookbooks he has written. The one I own and prize is *The Chef's Secret Cookbook* (1971, Quadrangle/New York Times Book Co.) in which the master, unlike many chefs, reveals his secrets—at least one and often several for each recipe.

In it, for example, you can learn how to cook green vegetables and have them retain their bright color: cook them uncovered and only to the crisp/tender stage. You can learn how to keep mixtures containing avocado from turning dark: place the pit in the mixture until serving time. When preparing brothy soups, the last bits of fat can be removed by wrapping a damp towel around ice cubes and skimming it lightly across the surface of the liquid. For page after page you can learn the chef's secrets for buying food, preparing it well, and creating tantalizing variations.

Naturally, it came to my mind that a master chef who is willing to share the secrets that "make" his recipes would probably have a few tips for success in the classroom. I say "naturally" because this is not the first occasion on which I've found an association between cooking and teaching—see, for example, "Students as Scrambled Eggs and Other Recipes for Teaching" [Chapter 8].

But Louis Szathmáry, a gracious man of many talents, has a busy life now as an international restaurant and hospitality consultant, and it's hard to catch up with him. So what follows is my own speculation on some of the secrets he *might* communicate if he took the time to focus on college teaching. To save space, I omit the recipes and offer only the secrets, one or two tips for each situation.

Lectures. Instead of delivering one long discourse, design your lecture as a series of short scenes, and devise ways at the end of each scene for students to work with the material, clarify it, convert it to long-term memory, and prepare for the next scene.

Discussions. Employ tactics that draw students into active involvement: tapes, film clips, slides, music, and other devices that present challenging images and stir emotions. Ask questions that stimulate response and interaction, such as "Why do you think that?" "What are the implications of Dana's suggestion?" "How do you react to Lee's comment?"

Basic laboratories. Design exercises that offer some personal excitement of accomplishment and discovery. Guide that process through carefully focused and phrased "consider questions" that require students to do a lot of thinking even for relatively simple procedure and outcomes.

Simulation, role-playing, and case studies. Construct cases, scenarios, and exercises based on actual situations in order to promote realistic experience. Insofar as possible write case studies in dialogue so that they may be played out by students.

Independent and field study. Provide periodic opportunities for a student to interact with others (students or faculty) in order to help distill meaning and significance from the experience.

Reading assignments. Instead of saying only "Read chapter X," suggest what students might look for and focus on; present questions that can be answered by the material to be read.

Examinations. Give individual feedback in writing to each student within one week of the examination.

Slide projection. Program slides in short sequences so that the room is darkened only for brief periods of time.

Overhead projection. Attach a 4x6 card to the mirror of the projector with masking tape. Flip this "light gate" down between transparencies so that the audience is never presented with a blank bright screen or an image that is no longer relevant to what students are being told.

Slides and transparencies. Limit information on each to no more than seven lines, with no more than seven words per line. Enlarge the material when making the transparency so that it nearly fills the screen when projected.

Television monitors. The optimum size of the screen is roughly equivalent to the number of people viewing it, as well as their distance from the screen. For example, probably no more than 12 people, sitting no farther than 12 feet from the monitor, can see well the image on a 12-inch screen.

Flip charts. Lightly line the sheets with pencil in advance in order to keep the material you write orderly.

Classes of any size. Strive to be able to call each student by name as soon as possible. For some courses, this can be facilitated by shooting Polaroid photos in groups of five or six, with students signing their names below their picture. For large classes, ask a different group of six to eight students to meet with you for a few minutes before each class so that you can get their reactions to assignments, course pace, etc.; in the process, you will learn a lot of names.

Presentations in general. As in the serving of food, presentation is very important to the reception of what you offer.

Pay attention to amounts, combinations, contrast, timing, color, and arrangement.

So, armed with these secrets, you will be an excellent teacher, right? Would you, armed with Louis Szathmáry's cooking secrets, be an excellent chef? In *The Chef's Secret Cookbook*, Chef Louis responds with a music metaphor: You could learn all the notes and the spectacular cadenzas from a great pianist, yet you yourself could not play a piece like Artur Rubinstein. "You see,...cooking is just like playing the piano—it needs talent, training, and practice," Louis says. "For this is the first secret of good cooking, the most important 'secret ingredients': constant training, constant practice, devotion, and joy in cooking. Yes, you must love cooking to do it right. If you do not, you just suffer."

I'll bet Louis Szathmáry might say much the same about college teaching. The most important "secret ingredients" are constant training, constant practice, devotion, and joy in teaching. You must love teaching to do it right.

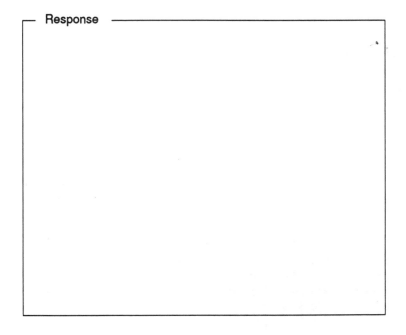

Response

26

There *Is* Life Beyond the Small Classroom

How I stopped worrying and learned to love the mass lecture.

For years I had enjoyed the luxury of teaching relatively small classes, rarely having to deal with more than 25 students in any course. I think that was due, in part, to the wisdom (or accident) of architects' designing classrooms of that size. (One of the Laws of Academe seems to be that the appropriate size for a class is a function of how many seats the custodian can fit into the room.)

For years I was able to know all my students by name within a couple of weeks of the start of the semester. It was easy to interact with everyone in a class; every student was only a few feet away from me. My energy could easily be transferred to the students. Their responses in turn prompted me to adjust my teaching to the needs of the moment. It was dynamic teaching. It was theatre-in-the-round in the best sense. It was the good life for both students and me.

Imagine my initial apprehension when at the end of my first year at a new university I was invited to teach a large lecture section of MAT 107, College Algebra. I was shocked to discover that those same architects who wisely designed intimate 25-person rooms for my mathematics classes also included in the building two impersonal lecture halls that each accommodated 220 students. Well, of course, those surely were meant for philosophy or history courses, but not for mathematics—right?

Wrong. In a world unexpectedly gone awry, I found that most of our pre-calculus courses were being taught in that setting.

When I say I was "invited" to teach a large lecture section, I use the correct word. It was not an invitation that carried a heavy expectation of compliance; I had a free option of saying Yes or No. But, since I am by nature a cooperative person (sometimes known as a soft-touch—or even a sucker), I suppressed the strong urge to run and hide; I did give the invitation serious consideration.

I reasoned with myself: Why not see how the other half lives—and teaches? It will be good experience. You've been wanting to work on your voice modulation and projection; this will give you a strong impetus to do so. Now is the time to check out all those things that you have advocated for making lectures more effective—remember what you said at the TA training seminar a couple of years ago? You can be innovative; why not see if you can incorporate some small-group techniques into large classes? It will be interesting. It will be challenging. You can write a paper about it.

I like challenges. I was convinced. I accepted.

Almost immediately I had regrets.

The course coordinator's secretary asked me to turn in my first three tests by July 15. July 15?—classes didn't even start until August 27! Each test was to consist of twelve questions. Each question was to have five multiple-choice answers. Tests were to be administered by student assistants in exactly 35 minutes in lab sections once a week; latecomers would not be allowed to take the quiz; make-ups were permitted in cases of illness, death or funerals, if properly certified. (The secretary and I eventually came to be good friends, but at that first moment I could never have predicted that it would happen.)

I had always prided myself on functional testing, focusing my evaluation on the process rather than just the answer, giving partial credit when warranted, providing extensive written feedback (both corrective suggestions and positive reinforcement) on returned examinations, using exam results diagnostically to indicate what I needed to stress more and then testing that on the next exam. Suddenly, I saw all this carefully conceived evaluation strategy being dumped from my program.

A day or so later, I peeked into the lecture room I would be using. Sure enough, there seemed to be at least 220 seats, beginning a few feet from the front wall and stretching onward and upward toward infinity. The chalkboards were on vertical tracks, but who beyond the tenth row could read what I wrote unless I did it in foot-high letters? I soon found the solution to this problem: a small space was carved out of the fourth row of seats; there sat a cart with a built-in overhead projector, together with a microphone and about a foot of shelf space. This niche was surrounded by a sea of student seats.

This would be the "stage" for my teaching activity. As one who recently has become captivated by the idea of the classroom as a dramatic arena, I found it terribly confining. Confining?—it was like a prison, a dungeon without walls.

As if I hadn't discovered enough, I sat in on a couple of the lectures of the 107 course in its summer term incarnation. There were only 60 or 70 students enrolled, but they scattered themselves evenly throughout the lecture hall (the Law of Uniform Diffusion at work, perhaps). The lecturer sat—yes, *sat*—at the lectern, writing equations on the blinding light table of the overhead projector, erasing them with a wet paper towel taken from a neatly-folded stack an inch or so high. "Any questions from the last test?" she asked of no one in particular, "Number 5, Yellow," came a voice from somewhere. Hardly looking up, the lecturer sketched out and explained a solution, noting that it was also the answer to Number 8, White. Much of the class was a matter of the instructor's transferring images through the projector to the large screen in front, with students dutifully reproducing them in notebooks.

As I left the room at the end of class, I asked a student how he liked the course. The unexpected reply gave me another shock: "Fine," he said, "It's very straightforward and clear; I know exactly what I have to do to make an A."

Well, I simply could not see myself sitting at that light table for three hours a week. I had never sat down in a math class in my life! Typically, I was all over the room; I used movement not only to punctuate my remarks but also to help energize students. I was constantly interacting with them, probing with questions, watching for discovery or bewilderment in their eyes, governing my activities by their reactions. The 107 mass lecture was not for me—no, not even considering that it counted double credits in my teaching load (compensation for hardship duty, I assumed).

On August 27, there I was, poised at the light table, launching the course. As I said, I like challenges. Besides, who was I to condemn the situation without giving it a try? I resolved to make the best of it, as inadequate as that might turn out to be.

The first class meeting, of course, was an utter disaster. I had hoped to run a shortened version of the opening-day drill that I had developed over the years: exhibiting what the course would be like, presenting interesting material, getting students to respond, making them feel at ease, revealing something of myself as a person, etc. I hastily scrubbed that plan, stumbled quickly through a few administrative details which were magnificently garbled by the malfunctioning microphone, and moved on to the placement test required of all 107 students. Even so, the process ran almost up to the start of the next class in that room. It was just about the worst way I could think of for beginning a course, and I feared that it might be weeks before I overcame the bad effects of it.

On the other hand, I reasoned (ever the optimist), almost anything I did from that point on would be an improvement.

I arrived at the second class armed with a stack of transparencies which contained the key elements of the material I would deal with; these were appropriately spaced so that I could add further details and examples as I went along. I plunged forward and before I knew it, the clock showed two minutes left and I had covered everything. Rarely before had I been able to pace myself so well in the first week of the academic year. It must have been due to the carefully laid-out pattern of transparencies. I asked for questions; there were none, and I dismissed the class. Right at that point I vowed to try to end each future lecture a bit early if I could and to end it on my own terms, rather than have the closing generated by shuffling feet and students' other preparations for leaving as the minute hand approached the top of the hour.

And, I did *not* sit down once! In order to remain standing, I had to hold the microphone, and that converted me into a one-armed teacher. Better to be one-armed and visible than to blend into the woodwork, I reasoned. I immediately launched a search for a good dynamic mike or a lavaliere that would restore me to a state of two-armedness. Alas, it was unsuccessful, even though I hunted all across campus. The best I was able to come up with was a clip-on mike that I repaired with a hearing-aid battery and kept as an emergency back-up; I had to use it only once, but it gave me needed security. I ended up by clamping the regular mike onto the front of the projection stand and adjusting the goose-neck to straight up in order to accommodate my standing position. Well, *almost* standing—I had to crouch just a tad, but the crick that developed in my neck usually went away within a few minutes after class. The Great Microphone Odyssey taught me another Law of Academe: Some of the simplest things are hard to change. (It is especially true when the change requires cooperation of persons elsewhere on campus who do not perceive why you need something that everyone else seems to get along fine without.)

That Law was reinforced when I attempted to arrange for a computer analysis of my quiz questions. There was no budget for score-sheets, university regs kept me from paying for them out of my own pocket, and besides, "a professor knows more about designing problems than a computer." I rejected a naive suggestion that I calculate discrimination and difficulty indices by hand, and I managed to "appropriate" a small supply of score-sheets from other (unnamed) sources. Another Law: Almost anything can be accomplished if you try hard enough, although the means may not be entirely legal.

But these are merely mechanical matters. What about enhancing learning?

One of the things I've learned about teaching is that the group of students in any particular course constitutes a unique entity. During the semester, the group evolves from a relatively formless mass into a distinct functional unit. In most courses, a point is reached where the group "jells" into this unit, a point where students and instructor feel comfortable working with each other. From then on, class meetings will flow rather smoothly, requiring only minimal attention to group maintenance. Until it happens, though, the instructor is being "tested" by students and must exert considerable effort toward bringing about the pectin effect. It is to be hoped that jelling occurs relatively early in the term; sometimes, of course, it never happens—unfortunately.

The point of all this is that a major element in the jelling action is the process of the instructor's getting to know the students, and vice versa. That involves the instructor's being willing to reveal self as a person. It also involves identifying students as individuals and discovering shared interests. It takes conscious effort. It takes time. It is rather difficult in large classes because of the numbers involved.

My colleagues with experience in the 107 course predicted that the only students I would get to know by name were those in the specific lab section to which I myself was assigned. I resolved (privately, of course) to prove them wrong, and I set targets of knowing at least 40% of the students by midterm and at least 80% by course end.

I found a few moments during the third class session to run a short get-acquainted exercise, adapted from one I'd used in other courses with good results. It was harder to assess its value in such a large class, but I felt sure that for some students their sense of comfort and identification with the class, and perhaps their responsiveness, was increased. The exercise certainly didn't hurt anything.

One of the best early moves I made was to negotiate for a TA to cover my own lab. That left me free to roam the corridor where the six labs were held—to be of help where I could, but also to be able on a casual basis to meet students on their way to and from lab. One week I filled in for an absent TA, and I found that I learned to associate names and faces for most of her 20-some students in the course of the hour. My retention of this information waned without periodic reinforcement, of course (the half-life of my memory seemed to be about two or three weeks). But, it was very useful to be able to call several students by name during subsequent lectures or when meeting them in the hallway.

Thereafter, I tried to spell my TAs in the labs whenever possible in an attempt to continue to improve my recognition of individual students. As a result, I could make lectures more and more personal to them. The ultimate satisfaction came one day when a student sitting well beyond my visual perception (even if I hadn't been blinded by the projector) called out a comment and I was able to identify her voice and to respond, "Yes, Laura, thanks for bringing that to my attention." When that began to happen more and more frequently I knew I was well on the way toward my goal of personalizing the course for students.

From the start, I was bothered that students in 107 rarely dropped by my office to seek assistance with their work. In part, this was due to our providing a tutorial lab staffed 44 hours per week by undergraduate students available to respond to questions. In my other courses, my informal contact with students provided me valuable feedback on how I was coming across in class. Sometimes in these office sessions I developed alternate strategies for solving and explaining problems. I missed these opportunities to gain information that I could convert into improved classroom instruction.

In partial compensation, I decided to establish a system of "spotters," students who would report to class a few minutes early and tell me of problems or concepts in the previous assignment that they found troublesome. I then tried to respond to these in the early part of my presentation that day. Occasionally, I would ask spotters questions about the course: Is there enough time for quizzes? Would late-afternoon help sessions be useful? Could problem solutions be posted for student review?— and the like.

A new set of spotters was designated for each class meeting, and the process became another way for me to relate to individual students. The system worked reasonably well (sometimes shy spotters came up to me after class and said that they didn't appear before class because they had no suggestions). Eventually, I initiated a modification of it in one of my other courses; I formed a screening committee to which students could recommend homework problems that might be reviewed in class.

Before long, I found that so many students were asking for problems to be worked in the mass lecture that my time for dealing with new material was being jeopardized. After seeking the advice of two or three sets of spotters, I started posting outside the lecture hall annotated solutions to selected problems from the assignments. These remained posted from quiz to quiz. My selection was based on questions that students asked me individually; if there were not enough gleaned by this method, I would choose a few additional ones. (And, I always went over one or two key problems each class, just as a matter of course.) It seemed to work well except for a few occasions when the solutions disappeared just before a quiz. The ultimate compliment came from a colleague in English who remarked eloquently one day, "That's a damn good idea!"

Then I did the same thing with quizzes, posting solutions and comments for all problems so that students could get immediate feedback as soon as they finished the quiz. Students reported this to be useful, too, so I felt it was worth the considerable extra effort.

Yet, an impersonal problem solution, even carefully annotated, was for some students not the answer to their difficulties in coping with the material; they needed to interact with a live person. I found a later afternoon time when a classroom was free· and began to hold weekly "clinic" sessions, times when I could help students cure some of their math ills.

Often this session turned into what I dubbed a "scrimmage"—students working at the chalkboard a variety of problems from the sections covered by the next quiz. Whether clinic or scrimmage, these sessions were opportunities to coach students toward improved performance. I had long advocated the coaching process as a good teaching strategy: positive performance is reinforced and incorrect performance is modified one step at a time.

Early on in the course, I made a standing offer to students: turn in homework and I'll be glad to review it (not for "extra credit," however) and return it with comments and suggestions. I extended the offer to quizzes, provided students did their work in an orderly, readable fashion (instead of randomly scattering calculations on scratch paper). Not many students took me up on these offers, but those who did reported great benefits from the procedure.

My initial concern about having over 200 students in the course proved unfounded. There were never more than 163 on the active roster nor more than 150 in any given session. As the semester advanced toward the midterm withdrawal date, normal attrition took over and the enrollment gradually declined. I regretted not having a shot at some of the students who were fading away, but the situation made it possible for me to focus more on those who remained. I put on a campaign to get students to move toward the front; some did, and the lecture became more like a smaller class, despite the size of the hall.

The organization I had imposed on myself through preparation of transparencies in advance—listing topics and key words, stating a problem and leaving space to work it, sketching axes in advance of graphing, etc.—surprisingly freed my mind to focus more on students in class and how they were reacting to the material. I found it possible to incorporate into lectures some interaction with students, albeit limited.

The transparencies represented a sequence of segments of the material, each of which roughly matched my students' pattern of attention to one topic. They established a pace for the course. (I found it interesting to listen to the almost coordinated flipping of notebook pages throughout the room each time I moved on to a new transparency.) After noting the success of dividing an hour's class into 8 to 12 distinct segments (though omitting the commercial breaks), I tried to do the same thing in my other courses; it worked well there, too.

Every once in a while, I punctuated changes of pace in my lectures by dropping in a cartoon character—for example, a Ziggy commenting on a problem solution ("Uncanny..."), a Peppermint Patty expressing smug satisfaction at having come up with the right answer or anguish at making a common mistake, a Snoopy lying atop his doghouse wishing everyone a relaxing weekend. My intent was to add a bit of warmth to lectures without being frivolous; after all, mathematics is not often a tremendously exciting subject at the service-course level. One student responded with her own contribution: Snoopy at his typewriter, pecking out The Great Novel, "It was a dark and stormy night...suddenly the quadratic formula rang out!" Two of my colleagues paid me compliments on the technique by asking to borrow several of the transparencies to use in their own mass lectures.

Not all of my initial concerns about testing disappeared, but I learned to adapt to the different kind of evaluation. I soon found that 12 full-fledged problems requiring computations often could not be completed by students in 35 minutes. Since my quizzes went into the computer several weeks in advance of their being given, there was a time lag before my modification of the quiz structure could take effect. In the meantime, I granted the students an extra five minutes per quiz.

Before long I determined that most of the week's material could be covered in less than 12 quiz questions. Since I was bound to a 12-question format, I focused the last several items on concepts that required mathematical comprehension, but little computation. I never did have to resort to a bunny question. (Well...I will admit that one graph *did* look somewhat like a small animal with large ears—but the question about it *was* a legitimate mathematical question.)

Eventually my composition of multiple-choice problems became more efficient, and the course coordinator and his secretary no longer had to hound me to get my quiz material in on time. I discovered one technique that helped speed up my production of quizzes: compose each item on a separate half-sheet of paper (also a good way to recycle old quiz answer sheets), then edit and sort the resulting sheets into appropriate orders for the two forms of the quiz. It was simple, yet surprisingly effective.

At about the middle of the term I made some assessments. I found that my apprehension and negative attitudes about the mass lecture had dissipated for the most part. The disaster of the first day was but a dim memory. I felt that almost all of the lectures had come off quite well—certainly much better than I had expected, and this was confirmed by reactions from a sample of students. I had been coming up with one good teaching innovation for every two or three classes—a pretty good batting average—and I looked forward to maintaining that rate for the remainder of the semester.

My special efforts to get to know students personally also paid dividends. By midterm I found that I knew nearly half of them by name, comfortably exceeding my goal of 40%. The jelling of the class into a true working unit seemed to have occurred just before midterm; I had worried that it would never occur at all. The students had changed from a sea of unknown, potentially hostile faces to a set of normal, friendly, everyday individuals (as I knew they really were). We had evolved into a group that was, for the most part, working toward a common goal.

Make no mistake about my expecting superb student evaluations at the end of the 107 course. I know I will not get them. There will be a mix of good and bad, and many indifferent, as many of us are used to getting. Some will respond favorably (as they already have) to efforts to make the course personal and even fun. Others will think it's a lot of foolishness and insist that I erred by not telling and force-feeding them every last thing to know. (There may be a few counterparts of that group among the readers of this article.) A goodly number will sandbag during the course and then use evaluations to reflect their likely grade—if they didn't score high on my challenging quizzes, for whatever reason, down go the evaluations of my teaching. Thus it ever was. Is another Law of Academe: Don't expect a whole lot of appreciation? (A corollary of that may be: No good deed or work goes unpunished!) I guess I'm willing to be content with knowing that I presented a course of integrity, tried to give it some of my best shots, and reached a significant number of students with my approach.

My colleagues will respond in a fashion similar to that of the students. Some have already voiced their compliments. On the other hand, I understand that at least one, who is somewhat of a departmental tyrant, has communicated (though not to me) that my methods and innovations are "inappropriate" in a course at that level—"That's not what that kind of student needs." It takes all kinds, even among teachers.

Do I have any advice for would-be teachers of mass lectures? Yes, but be sure to know that I speak from limited experience. First, recognize that a certain amount of uniformity is necessary and probably even desirable for large, multi-section courses; that's the nature of activities that become institutionalized. Accommodate it, live with it, don't fight it. Save your energy for those things that can be changed and hope that you have the wisdom to distinguish those from the impossible missions.

Second, have the courage to be innovative in your teaching—you can change that—and do your damndest to produce a functional, dynamic course that still recognizes and respects students as individuals of integrity. You may or may not be able to use my specific innovations, but I hope they will stimulate you to seek your own.

There definitely are benefits to be gained from teaching mass lectures: reaching more students, accepting and meeting a challenge to the best of your ability, pushing your creativity to the utmost. I even found an unusual and welcomed dividend from my new teaching mode: an environment free from clouds of chalk dust. My lungs gave me a vote of appreciation!

Now I'm facing the remaining several weeks of the semester with renewed enthusiasm. I'm even regretting my decision early in the term (when such things are required) to decline an opportunity to teach another mass lecture next semester. Maybe I'll have another shot at it next fall, if they'll still have me. In a couple of months I'll go back to the familiar and comfortable pattern of having all small classes. But, I'll go back with some new ideas that, surprisingly, I'll translate from my experiences in the large lecture. I guess anyone—even a teacher—can draw lessons from any situation if the mind is set right.

Thus, I am brought to the final paragraph of this narrative. My mind is now conditioned to conjuring up one last transparency, just as at the end of a 107 lecture. What would I communicate to those who want to try a mass lecture or who want to renew their approach to mass lectures with innovative techniques? In my mind's eye, I see a small figure in a baseball cap, standing on a pitcher's mound, surrounded by his buddies. They're all shouting encouragement to him: "You can do it, Charlie Brown, you can do it!"

┌─ Response ───

│

└──

27

The Secret Life of Professor Mitty

This is what it's all about, Mitty thought. Teaching really is a noble profession. It's a chance to enrich students' lives, an opportunity to affect eternity.

"...an unusually difficult task to meld the diverse viewpoints and factions of the faculty, but you were able to bring your unique talents to bear on the process and carry it to a most successful conclusion. Our program with the revised canon will be a model for many years to come. Already other institutions are basing their curriculum revisions on ours. Your work will certainly have an impact throughout higher education." Alfred Mitty's eyes lifted from the president's letter and glanced out the open window at a campus taking on the fresh green of early April. The strains of music floated through the air—the university orchestra rehearsing for the forthcoming academic festival. Professor Mitty's eyes misted over.

He returned to the final paragraph of the letter in his hands: "Let me also take this opportunity to congratulate you on your paper, 'Everyday Implications of Mathematical Anti-rings and Semi-manifolds,' that received the award from the Academy. It's a remarkable exposition of the practical application of your research, something that often is not considered in your field. Even I, a mere classicist, was able to comprehend its scientific basis." The letter was signed, "Warmly, Marcia."

But there was more. Penned at the bottom was a post-script: "Charles and I are having a small dinner party for the visitors from Moscow next month. I hope you and your charming wife can join us. I'll have my secretary call you with further details..."

The jangle of the class-change signal brought Alfred Mitty back to stark reality. He fingered the handful of memos and brochures he had extracted from his mailbox: the usual assortment of publishers' notices, announcements of three committee meetings, the latest drafts of the departmental mission statement and outcomes assessment guidelines, and notes from two students petitioning to take make-ups for Friday's exam. He put the student notes in his briefcase; he gave the rest a brief glance before dropping it onto the overflowing wastebasket that was the ultimate fate of most of the department's mail. It teetered for a moment before slipping off to the pile on the floor. Mitty left the office and walked slowly down the corridor.

...students greeted him warmly as he strode toward class. "Good morning, Professor Mitty." "Hello, Professor M." "Morgen, Herr Professor" (that from a student who knew Mitty spoke several languages and who tried a different one each time they met). Mitty returned the greetings with a nod of the head and a shy smile.

"Good morning, Emm," one of the more daring said. Mitty nodded and smiled, but chuckled inwardly; he knew the students' little secret of privately calling him "M" or "Emm"—in reference to the way he initialed notes on papers he returned to them or to the occasional "emm" that still crept into his lectures, a remnant of his ploy to cure the sprinkling of "uhs" that marred his exposition in his early teaching days. Students now flocked to his courses (rather unusual for mathematics), and calling him M had become their sign of affection for him. His only acknowledgment of their custom was wearing his Michigan varsity sweater to final examinations.

A student caught up to Mitty and walked beside him. "Professor M, I want to thank you for your suggestion on my research project in economics. That was the elusive idea that had been escaping me for weeks. Your comments will help me have my senior thesis finished on time. I'm grateful for your assistance."

"I'm glad it's working out for you," Mitty replied. "But it wasn't much. I'm glad I could be of a little help."

"You were a *great* help," she said. "See you in seminar tomorrow afternoon." Her hand brushed his sleeve with a light filial touch as she turned away from him. "Thanks again, Emm," she called as she rushed off.

A warm glow came over him. Ah, youth! This is what it's all about, Mitty thought. Teaching really is a noble profession. It's a chance to enrich students' lives, an opportunity to affect eternity, as his friend from Cambridge, recently designated Distinguished Professor, so aptly put it. Mitty rejoiced again at his decision some 15 years ago to reject that high-paying job in industry. That was just a job; this is work, his Life's Work. As he turned into his classroom he hummed a Brahmsian motif— *gaudeamus igitur, juvenes dum sumus...*

The students were scattered here and there in the room. Why so few today? Mitty wondered as he shuffled his books and papers at the front desk. A chemistry exam this afternoon? No, that was last week. Hmm. Oh, it's only three or four days until spring break, he thought; that's probably why—they're on their way to Lauderdale or Cancun. He pondered whether to give his planned presentation to the loyal and/or impecunious few or to modify it, since he'd probably have to repeat portions of it after break.

...before Mitty began his lecture a student stood and addressed him. "Professor Mitty, three of us spent the weekend working over the theorems you mentioned in your last lecture. We think we've discovered a new slant on one of them. With your permission, we'd like to take 10 or 15 minutes to present our ideas to the rest of the class."

"Certainly, Mr. Briggs, certainly. Please do," Mitty replied and sat down. Isn't it amazing, he thought, how students will take responsibility for their own learning if you only give them encouragement and the opportunity? The activity proposed by Briggs now occurred so frequently in Mitty's courses that he always built some flexible time into the design of his classes in order to accommodate it...

Mitty sighed and dismissed class ten minutes early. There's no need to belabor his points to the handful of half-awake students lolling in their seats. He could tell that their minds were in other places—on the beaches, in the bars, somewhere. He quietly gathered his papers and turned to leave the room.

Briggs was waiting at the door. "That stuff, you know, on historical perspective—that's not going to be on the exam, is it?" he asked. "Like, after all, this is a math course—we shouldn't have to be responsible for history and junk like that."

...Mitty sat at his computer, his hands poised impatiently over the keyboard. Anti-rings and semi-manifolds, he mused, anti-rings and semi-manifolds. Anti-fields? No. Semi-groups? No; that's already been studied. Tantalizingly, the concept danced just out of the grasp of his searching mind. Suddenly there came a voice out of the past, the voice of Herr Mann, his calculus professor, long since gone to his just reward: *"Man muss immer umkehren."* Of course! Turn it around! Why hadn't he thought of that before? Semi-rings... Yes! And anti-manifolds... Mitty's fingers flew over the keys. The screen filled with numbers and symbols. Of course! *Semi*-rings and *anti*-manifolds! An entirely new area of research...

Mitty placed another paper on the stack of graded exams, leaned back and closed his eyes, trying to make his mind go blank. He had no success, no relief. A burning laser-sharp voice still commanded: If you finish this batch before six o'clock, you'll have to take only two sets home with you tonight. He forced his eyes open, took a deep breath, and re-sharpened his green pencil. The clock-radio on his desk showed 4:26 and presented yet another Kenny Rogers tune. Mitty blew dust from the tip of the pencil and reluctantly attacked another paper.

...the rich tones of the President's voice soared over the crowd of several thousand assembled for the academic festival on this warm May afternoon. "No occasion in all my years here has carried the pleasure that the next event brings me. Our university could receive no higher honor. One of our faculty, one of our very own, one of my dearest friends has received a distinction, richly deserved though never coveted, that comes to only one of the tens of thousands of dedicated teachers in our nation's colleges and universities. I present to you someone you all know and love: Alfred Mitty, Professor of the Year."

A wave of emotion washed over Mitty. The happenings of the next few minutes faded in and out of focus, as in a magical dream. The berobed marshalls coming to escort him to the front. The audience rising to its feet. Shouts of "Bravo! Bravo!" resounding over the thunderous applause of the crowd. His mounting the three steps to the podium. The orchestra playing Brahms. The 200-voice choir singing, *"Alma mater floreat, quae nos educavit..."*

Response

28

Students on the Line

Grading would be a lot less difficult if it were only a matter of numbers.

Professor Harry Aguilar sat at his desk, entering the last of the exam scores into the computer. The glow of the screen and the circle of light from the desk lamp were all that brightened his study at this late hour. "Classics 'til Dawn" had just begun on WUFM—Tchaikovsky's *Sixth Symphony* softly accompanied his end-of-term ritual: processing final grades.

Stevens, the computer prompted. Harry entered *83*. *Stevens 411 total*, the computer responded.

Hey, she's really improved, Harry thought.

Stottlemeyer ... 69 ... 375 total.

Aaughh—Bill fell down on the final.

Trammell ... 78 ... 363 total.

Not bad. He may get his C yet.

Turpin ... 76 ... 420 total.

OK. But I expected a little better from him.

Walker ... 62 ... 395 total.

Oh-oh. Not so good ...

Winston ... 92 ... 478 total.

Yeah! 'Way to go! She's still at the top of the heap.

That's it, Harry said to himself. Let's look at the statistics. He entered a command and the screen filled with figures.

Harry studied them. *Range 283-478*. Not bad for a maximum 500 total. *Median 385. Mean 383. Standard deviation 52.* Good; most of the total scores are within two standard deviations of the mean. Let's get a distribution and see where the breaks are.

He entered a command and the computer printed out a distribution of the totals, ordered from high to low.

Yep, Winston's a clear A—and three others are not far behind her, Harry observed. Nice gap between 460 and 439. Clear distinction there. That's where the A/B line will be. It's good to have clean breaks between categories—no arguments that way.

He drew a line below 460.

Let's see what's happening at the bottom of the distribution. Loman 283 and Bivins 285—those are clear failures. And Jenkins 290, too. Poor guy; he just never had a chance. He was in 'way over his head. Looks like Williams 308 will probably be the lowest D.

He drew a line below 308.

And there's another break above 342—that'll be the C/D separation. Not too many D's this time; good. Whew ... you made your C, Trammell, but not with much room to spare.

He drew another line between 361 and 342.

Let's go back to the Bs. The top one's 439 ... then 434 and 433 ... a couple of 428s ... 420 ... 414 ... 411 ... 407 ... 401 ... 396 ... 395 ... 392 ... hmm, the biggest gap's been only eight points, too tight for a cut ... 385 ... 380 ... 375 ... Oh-oh. Should be a break in there somewhere. It's a long reach from 439 down to 361. Gotta be a B/C line somewhere ... where is it? Hmm ... should be at about 400 or 410. That would be about 80%.

Harry stared at the screen.

But the points really don't tell it all, he thought.

There's Walker at 395. Jeannie's grades were really up there early in the term, but she tumbled badly. Missed quite a few classes lately. I wonder why. She might not make the cut.

Mike Miller 414. Good ol' Mr. Nice Guy. Pretty good fullback, too. Easy going. Always goofin' around, but never any trouble. I wish I could motivate him to be more serious and get down to work. His academic performance doesn't deserve a lot of consideration. But he managed to hit the final pretty well, just like last term.

There's Ed Jackson 407. He's back after being out for several years. Doesn't speak up much, but when he does it's really solid. Comes to all the help sessions. Steady Eddie.

And Ken Greenburg 380. This is a tough course for nonmajors. Ken works like hell and he contributes a lot in class.

Deserves a break more on effort than anyone else. But just can't seem to hit the tests. He's so worried he called twice today to see if I had finished grading.

Right in the middle there is Kate Saunders 401. She did a great job in the lead in Players' production this term. I think she's got a lot of potential. But she's the quietest one in the class. Still water runs deep?

Josie Muñiz is down there in the 380s with Ken. On the basis of points alone, she's another good candidate for a C. But she's highly motivated, and I'm sure once she got going she'd excel. Makes good use of my conference hours. One of the most deserving of the bunch. She needs the grades to get into Ed School. The way she's dealt with her own disability would make her great in special education. Her parents will probably pull her out of college if she doesn't get into the Education program this year.

Harry scanned the scores again and breathed a deep sigh.

Where's the cutoff? Or should they all get Bs? Naw. Maybe all Cs? A C really isn't so bad; it's average. But I guess it makes a big difference to a student.

It's agonizing at end-of-term. Grading would be a lot less difficult if it were only a matter of numbers.

Sometimes I wish I didn't know anything about my students. But I do. They're all lives-in-progress. What I decide can really affect them. Maybe it shouldn't, but it does.

I know I can record any grade I want to, even arbitrarily; I really don't have to justify anything. But that's not the point. I just can't blow it off like that.

Harry rubbed his eyes, leaned back in his chair, and sighed again.

Whoever said teaching would be satisfying and rewarding *and fun* sure wasn't thinking about making out final grades ...

29

Advice for New Teachers

Will teaching become easier and easier with time and experience? Yes and No.

> *Teaching really isn't that hard. And with a little experience, you'll find that it gets easier and easier. Once you get the hang of it and learn the basics it doesn't take a lot of effort to be a good teacher. Be careful that you don't overprepare. If you know the material, it'll just come natural to you and you'll enjoy it.*

That's the gist of a comment I heard recently. I think it was said in all honesty and sincerity. As with most advice, there are seams of truth in it. But those seams are overburdened with misleading information.

If the advice sounds familiar to you, you may have heard pieces of it from a TA supervisor, from a department chair, or at new-teacher orientation. Maybe even you yourself have passed it along to a new teacher, as I know I have. Since the advice is so pervasive, it's worth examining in greater depth.

I think the reason we hear such advice so often is that we recognize that new teachers are somewhat apprehensive about facing their classes. Well-intentioned veteran teachers want to reassure the novices. There's nothing wrong in that.

But the truth is that almost *all* teachers experience apprehension when facing a new class, a new course, or a new teaching assignment—or in trying out something new in class. Just as with novice teachers, it's an apprehension born out of the unknown and born out of a desire to do well. For a few, apprehension may disappear in time. For most of us, though, it doesn't; it only becomes modified with experience.

Teachers become comfortable with that tension as a result of facing and handling it regularly. They find that once they are in the classroom and the day's activities get underway, the butterflies calm down. As each course progresses, the class begins to jell and teacher and students get on a roll [see "Getting a Class to Jell," Chapter 3]. But the feeling never goes away completely. And by recognizing that it's normal, we're able to deal with it more easily. In one sense, it's a good kind of stress that keeps us on our toes and continuing to try to do our best.

But be assured that there will still be an occasional bad day. Any of us can hit a real downer, perhaps through no fault of our own. Just never have two in a row. Ensure that the next class meeting is so good that it more than makes up for the temporary lapse.

Will learning basic teaching techniques and being well grounded in the material reduce the effort of teaching? The answer is both Yes and No—but more the latter. Certainly, knowing material and techniques is important in doing an effective teaching job, but that's just the beginning. You could learn scales and all the basics of playing the piano, along with all the notes of a sonata, but that would not be sufficient to play the piece well. It requires refinement of technique, emotional investment, and practice to the point of proficiency—and even then the performance can always get better. A concert presentation may seem effortless to an audience, but it is the culmination of a long process of preparation by the artist.

So it is with teaching. For example, you may easily comprehend the principles of asking questions that elicit student response, but the subtle skills of applying the principles in a wide variety of circumstances comes only with constant effort. Teaching is a complex process that involves the imaginative integration of many particulars, not the application of simplistic formulas. Each class is different. Each student is different. Each moment is different. Therefore, each instructional move is unique. And by the time one feels comfortable in applying some techniques, one discovers other new things to try and the process of mastery begins anew.

It's commonly said that new teachers tend to overprepare, but I've never seen any definitive evidence of this. I suppose, by definition, overdoing anything is unnecessary and undesirable. And we can argue that there is value in spontaneity in instructional activity, as well as value in flexibility to adjust to unforeseen circumstances that may arise. The line between well-prepared and overprepared is often fine and difficult to determine. It's a judgment call that improves with experience. Good teachers have bad dreams all their lives about arriving at class unprepared; in large part those dreams reflect the subconscious anxiety that keeps such negative situations from actually happening.

My experience—and others verify it—suggests that the conscientious teacher is likely to *increase* preparation for teaching as time rolls on. I can recall in my first teaching years going to each class with a single 3x5 card containing on one side the next day's assignment and my notes (prepared the night before). Since I thought mathematics could be laid out so orderly, it seemed that all I needed was a set of words to trigger my mind and the rest would follow logically. By contrast, in my most recent classroom experiences—some 30 years later—I laid out my general plan and assignments for each three or four week period between exams and distributed an information sheet to students.

At the end of each week, I'd review my plan for the next week. Two nights before a given class, I'd sketch out a "script" of several instructional scenes, complete with specific examples and the various strategies I'd employ. I tried to articulate my plan with the status of the class meeting we had earlier that day. The next night I'd make a few modifications and fill in additional details. For 10 or 15 minutes before class I'd do a final fast-speed mental run-through of what I wanted to accomplish and how I'd do it; in essence, I was getting myself in character for that class. Once in the classroom, I'd hardly glance at my three or four pages of notes because almost everything was fixed in my head by that time. Often I'd change the course of instructional activity in mid-class if circumstances warranted it. All that's a far cry from my early days with 3x5 cards.

Occasionally I've observed a colleague walk into class without notes, open a book, work the problems from the day's assignment, and when the bell rings walk out leaving the students to the next assignment contained on a sheet photocopied from last year's syllabus. It's very distressing to see teaching apparently taken so lightly. That kind of travesty seems to me to be the epitome of professional irresponsibility.

I'm not suggesting that good teaching requires an *enormous* amount of time, preparation, and effort. But it does require *substantial* amounts of those quantities, as befits the role that for most of us is the centrum of our professional lives. Doing one's best through the ever-enduring process of searching, winnowing, maturing, refining, and perfecting is the height of our ethical responsibility.

Some aspects of teaching do get easier and easier as we get the hang of it. But as most of us grow as teachers we become aware of the complexity of the role. We perceive and accept the greater teaching challenges that we encounter. We match the challenges with more and more effort. We are reinforced by the joy and exhilaration of facing them and succeeding. We glow in the satisfaction of seeing lights turn on in our students' eyes, from the rush that comes from knowing we've conducted a class session well. We do indeed enjoy this noble enterprise called teaching. May you enjoy it also.

Response

30

Workshop Gleanings

Reflecting on what has been gained in a workshop or classroom experience is a beneficial process for both participants and presenter.

I'm returning from Atlantic Canada after a series of workshops on college teaching. Due to ground fog and air traffic delays at Logan International Airport, my plane at this moment is entering an extended holding pattern, 30 to 40 miles off Boston. I'm granted unexpected free time.

From my lofty perspective of 16,000 feet, I search the seascape below for Cape Ann, Cape Cod, or other points of land that might identify just where we are. Similarly, the perspective of time turns my mind to scanning the previous several days for things that might mark the focus, definition, and value of the workshop experiences.

The latter process is stimulated in part by some paragraphs I've just read. In them, workshop participants reflect on their experience and its meaning for them, particularly considering what new activity they might undertake as a result of the workshop. During the final session, these responses were collected, redistributed, and then read aloud in an exercise I call Hearing Every Voice.

Here are excerpts from a few of the paragraphs:

> *This seminar has given me some ideas about how to improve my teaching, but more importantly it has given me confidence to take risks in the classroom.*

I feel that improvement of my teaching skills is not only possible, but probable, as steps toward improvement can be small, and many small steps can lead to a large change.

One thing that I learned today is that some of the things I often criticize myself for are also some of the things I don't value much—so now I have permission not to focus on them.

We are encouraged to do research, research, research; but what really matters is our ability to communicate our ideas, our thought processes, etc., on to the next generation so they can experience the same excitement and joy of learning that we experienced.

I articulated some of my values, attitudes, and present behaviors, which made me more self-aware. I am now considering some different approaches to how I educate my students. And I also received some reinforcement that some of the things I do are on the right track. This is a good starting point for change!

I was challenged to consider that there is more to teaching than getting by or getting through the material. In order to affect the lives of my students and fully facilitate their learning, I must have the willingness and stick-to-it-iveness to do what it takes to rise to new heights. I must create a class environment that is creative, interesting, and which challenges students to put their best into their learning and to come away fully excited about their own potential.

I became more aware of a contradiction between my values and my behavior...I am looking at ways to remove the contradiction.

The workshop has been an excellent booster and stimulus to try all those things I dream about to improve teaching quality and effectiveness... As always, hearing the frustrations and obstacles of my colleagues assures me that I'm not alone and that there is hope.

Discovering that there is creativity in the chemistry department and low managerial skills in the management fields, but humor in all—and a little cynicism—all added to the sense of where one person in one department in one institution fits into the Greater Universe. And yes, a sense of community was high on my list of goals/values!

[Today's workshop] has also made me want to go and try these ideas very soon in my next teaching sessions. I can't wait to start!

If the workshops have been so beneficial to the participants, I reason, perhaps they have been beneficial to me also. Thus, I am putting this tranquil time spent circling over the ocean to good use by reflecting on what I myself gleaned from the workshops.

The workshops verified for me once again that there are many faculty members who take their teaching seriously and seek to perform ever better in the classroom. I find that gratifying.

These dedicated faculty members seem almost starved for opportunities to talk with their colleagues about teaching. Such conversations seem to motivate them, focus their energies, and lead to resolve to incorporate new ideas into their work. It suggests that universities might well make more concerted efforts to provide for increased dialogue on teaching. This need not necessarily be in organized workshops. Dialogue could occur in monthly luncheons, study clubs, departmental groups, and even between pairs of faculty members who meet informally to share their ideas.

Faculty members working with each other represent collectively a far greater resource than a workshop leader operating as an individual. My trust in that resource has been reinforced, and I'll continue to design into workshops as much cooperative effort as I can. In many classrooms, too, students collectively represent a useful resource that can be tapped.

Given the opportunity, participants can tie together the threads of a workshop much better than I can. For example, in an exercise such as Hearing Every Voice, my best move is to let the power of that summary stand and not risk either up-staging it or diminishing it by my intervention. The lesson applies as well to a variety of classroom activities where the eloquence of empowered students breaks forth.

I've found again that the best laid schemes o' mice and men—and women—gang aft a-gley (to quote from one of my favorite poets). But the challenge thus laid before presenters and teachers may produce some of our finest moments.

For example, for a workshop on effective use of discussion groups I submitted a sketch of how I wanted tables and chairs in the room to be arranged in order to facilitate breaking up into small groups. I arrived on the scene to find that I'd been assigned to a brand-new "state-of-the-art" lecture hall: ten tiers of seating with fixed desks. Instead of throwing up my hands and letting the room control me, I devised ways for participants to spend a large portion of our time together working in groups of three or six.

This serendipitous example spoke better about how to cope with potential physical constraints to discussions than anything I could have said. We need not let the conventional wisdom of facility planners restrict our educational design. (As an aside, I wonder how often architects have designed "state-of-the-art" discussion rooms.)

Further, we should be careful that our own instructional design does not blind us to modifications and alternatives that might better accomplish our task. A suggestion acquired one day, after conducting a workshop with 60 participants, led to remarkably improved variations in the Hearing Every Voice exercise when it was used the next day with a group of over 100.

And in preparing for one workshop on discussions, I found myself responding to new ideas and sketching out design revisions up to ten minutes before the beginning. The result turned out to be the smoothest session of the week, and the satisfaction of having facilitated such an outcome was exhilarating.

The lessons: Plan well in advance, but always keep working over ideas. Be flexible and watch for opportunities for improvement. And then have the courage to risk something new, having faith in your capabilities to bring it off with success.

Throughout my reflection I'm aware that my helping others focus on enhancing their teaching effectiveness in turn helps me focus on enhancing the effectiveness of my own efforts. That focusing process drives us all forward in teaching, rising to new heights and gaining new satisfactions.

Just now the crackling of the plane's intercom startles me out of my musing. The captain announces that she's been cleared from the holding pattern and that we'll soon be on the ground in Boston. Before long I'll be back in the bustle of baggage, customs, and all that.

But mentally and emotionally, I'll be at 16,000 feet, still held high by the experiences of the week.

┌─ Response ───┐
│   │
│   │
│   │
│   │
│   │
│   │
│   │
│   │
│   │
│   │
│   │
│   │
│   │
└───┘

31

How One Teaches
Speaks So Loudly...

*Teachers might well examine the implications of
classroom structure, methods, and behavior—
including the effect on what we teach and what
students learn.*

Recently, I was in a group of a dozen faculty members having
lunch and talking about teaching. Many of us teachers yearn to
share ideas about our work with others, but seldom do we take
the time to do so. This day, on this small campus, we were doing
it. On this particular occasion, we focused on the relationship
between how we teach and what we teach.

We talked about how the structure of learning activities
sometimes can drown out the material of a course and, indeed,
drown out learning itself. We talked about the cacophony of a
professor's lecturing students about the discussion nature of a
course. We talked about how elaborate anti-cheating procedures can undermine attempts to build trust in the classroom.
We observed how our sitting in a circle encouraged talking with
each other, but how the arrangement in a typical classroom
reinforces only a series of teacher-student two-person dia-
logues. We talked about how various postures one takes—
standing behind a podium, walking around in front of the room,
sitting at the front, sitting in a circle with students—convey
different ideas about authority and the value of students' contributions. We talked about how trying to maintain a "value-
free" classroom itself communicates very strongly the value

that values are not important in life. We talked about how extensive clarification of evaluation procedures may inadvertently overemphasize grades.

Clearly there is an important relationship between process and content, between style and substance, between *forme et fond* (as the French would say). The two must be in harmony, not dissonance. And there may be great differences between what we intend to communicate and what we actually communicate.

Finally, each of us at the luncheon discussion took out a sheet of paper and completed the sentence stem, "*How* one teaches speaks so loudly..." Here's a sample of the responses:

How one teaches speaks so loudly that the words one speaks are hardly audible.

How one teaches speaks so loudly that it might be necessary to teach more softly.

How one teaches speaks so loudly—how one's students learn must have a voice too.

We also identified what each of us would do as a result of the day's conversation—attend to better openings for classes and courses, monitor our nonverbal behavior more closely, share with our students our attitudes and our approaches to the subject, etc.

I do not give a thorough report on the responses, because I don't want to preclude readers' sharing in this activity and gaining for themselves benefits similar to what we gained. You may want to complete for yourself the sentence "*How* one teaches speaks so loudly..." and then list two or three things that you'll do in your teaching as a result of considering the topic. Perhaps you might ask some colleagues to do the same, then talk it over with each other. I think it would be well worth the few minutes it takes.

32

Omnia Mutantur

An unusual homecoming triggers some thoughts on change, growth, art, teaching, life, and courage.

In one's mid-life, opportunity occasionally arises to drop back briefly into earlier incarnations—reliving half-forgotten experiences, awakening dormant friendships, and reveling in the spirit (if not quite the passions) of long years ago.

So it was last Thanksgiving when seven of us gathered for a reunion in the town in southern Ohio where we first started teaching together "over 20 years ago," as one tactfully described it. (The fact that the university's enrollment had grown fourfold is one indication of the real passage of time.)

The more things change, the more they stay the same? To be sure, the years had produced some physical changes in us (primarily in weight and pate). But I was struck by how each of us had retained certain "trademark" characteristics of speech and laughter, not to mention gait, posture, and other nonverbal behaviors. At the poker game (the ostensible excuse for our homecoming), we each fell into the same roles we played in earlier days. There was the same camaraderie, the same esprit, as though no years had intervened. (And I suspect there were the same winners and losers.)

Or is it perhaps: The more things stay the same, the more they change? In the old days, six of us were smokers; now none are. In the old days, all of us drank beer throughout a poker evening; this time, the drinks of choice seemed to be diet sodas and ice water. What a healthy bunch we turned out to be!

Or could it be: The more things change, the more they change? That thought occurred to me the day after the reunion when I visited David Hostetler, one of my poker buddies, at his sculpture studio on Coolville Ridge. The two us go back much farther than just our first teaching days; we were good friends in junior high and high school, where we shared lockers, classes, sundry escapades (best left unmentioned here), and on occasion even girl friends.

In those early days, David and I were together in art classes, and we seemed to function on similar levels. The ensuing years saw us take different paths. He pursued art as a career and has achieved significant international recognition. I followed mathematics and put art to the side except for a little photography in odd moments. I wondered about the divergence.

Certainly talent is a factor. David has superb capability in his field; he has an artist's eye—a unique perception and vision.

But I think I have a bit of artistic perception, too. (It shows up in my photography, I'm told.) What keeps me from pursuing art? I visit museums and view contemporary paintings and sculpture. And I think to myself, I could do things like that if I tried. But I never do. What makes the difference between a real artist and a mere dabbler or a wannabe?

I look at David. He has dedication, commitment, persistence—a sense of mission. It's an act of faith for him to chisel away at a log of rare wood for days on end. He has to *believe* that he's making just the right decisions that will result weeks or months later in a work of art that meets his high standards. Knowing that half of that expensive wood will become chips and shavings on the studio floor emphasizes the importance of faith.

But there's more. David has a courage that goes far beyond mere confidence—courage to devote himself to his art, courage to present publicly the expression of his emotional inner self, courage to risk. It's an audacious courage. He calls his work *art*, and he signs it as his own. He dares to stake his existence on his talents.

And that audacious courage, I think, is the essential quality that separates the great artist from the pretenders or those of us who never get very far beyond a beginning.

What, you might wonder, does this have to do with teaching? (After all, that's what this column is supposed to be about, my editor tells me.) A lot, I think.

Teaching, too, requires dedication, commitment, and persistence. Teachers must have a sense of mission. We must have faith that our efforts will bring results weeks, months, even years later—results that meet our goals, expectations, and standards. And the results in education often are much harder to perceive and assess than in art.

But to become really good teachers, as to become really good artists, we must have audacious courage to devote ourselves to *our* art, to express ourselves and our emotions publicly, and—especially—to risk new things, knowing the real possibilities of not always succeeding the first time.

We must search for new approaches to teaching and try innovations in the classroom. We must dare to throw away our old notes for a course and start anew. We must share with our students our excitement and our willingness to innovate. We must enlist students more in the process of their own learning. We must share our ideas and enthusiasm with our colleagues. We might even seek out and teach a course we have never taught before—or, better yet, team teach with a colleague, perhaps even in a different field.

My visit with my sculptor friend taught me more lessons.

David has become a well-known, well-exhibited, and especially well-paid artist. Some of his current pieces sell for much more than the combined annual salaries the two of us received when we started teaching together. He has a summer gallery on Nantucket, and a recent book on his career, *Hostetler, the Carver*, is enjoying good sales. So what is he doing at the moment when many colleagues our age are preparing to wind down their careers?

Though David is retired from teaching art at the University, he is building on his place in the country a large gallery that itself will be an artistic masterpiece. He's moving into an exciting new abstract style that I think will carry him to pinnacles even higher than he's already attained.* He's still finding and bringing out what's inside him. He's excited. He's happy. He's working harder than ever. He's growing. He's on top of the world.

---

*Five years after I recounted the events in this article, David Hostetler is completing a major commission for a large sculpture "Duo," that will occupy a prominent position at the entrance of the new Trump International Tower in New York City.

"Grow or die," I comment to him, thinking of how some people of our vintage already are succumbing to the front-porch-rocker syndrome.

"Change or die. Art follows life. This is still prime time," he flashes back at me.

Both artists and teachers remain vital only so long as they discover new modes of expression, progress from where they are to a more advanced state, and continue toward fulfillment. Few of us ever really exhaust our full potential.

I think of some lines whose author is unknown to me, and I realize the important ideas they express for all of us:

> *If you always believe*
> *What you have always believed,*
> *You will always feel*
> *The way you have always felt.*

> *If you always feel*
> *The way you have always felt,*
> *You will always think*
> *The way you have always thought.*

> *If you always think*
> *The way you have always thought,*
> *You will always do*
> *What you have always done.*

> *If you always do*
> *What you have always done,*
> *You will always get*
> *What you have always gotten.*

> *If there is no change,*
> *There is no change.*

I think also of the prayer for "courage to change the things we can change, the serenity to accept what we cannot change, and the wisdom to know the difference."

And I'm reminded of a saying from Roman antiquity: *Omnia mutantur, nos et mutantur in illis.* Indeed, all things change, and we change with them. Of course, we can float adrift in the tide of change, or we can respond actively by seizing the opportunity for growth and development. The choice is ours to make.

Thus I reflect on my Thanksgiving experience and the memories it has stirred. And I wonder what art there still may be within me, waiting to be brought out.

I gaze into my backyard, where rest some large sections of a tree cut down last summer. I don't need more firewood, so there's no point in expending energy to split the pieces. The wood is too good to discard or let rot. In my mind the logs begin to take on carved new shapes. My eye sees them composed one on top of another, creating an abstraction of nature. I muster up a bit of courage, and I go to the garage to get some tools and start working—and continue growing.

Response

33

Questions for Teachers

All too seldom do we turn important questions on ourselves, reflecting on them and discussing them with our colleagues.

New York Times Best Seller #1. Over one million in print! The fake gold seal on the cover boldly declaimed the popularity and implied importance of the *Book of Questions* by Gregory Stock (New York: Workman, 1987, 206 pp., $4.95).

Publishers' promotional ploys such as this rarely attract inveterate bookstore browsers like me. I might never have given the *Book* a second glance if my son and daughter-in-law hadn't snapped it up to use in their teaching.

Three hours later, after Karl and Jill each had given it a quick reading, my curiosity was aroused. When no one was looking, I picked up Stock's best-seller and found that it consisted entirely of 417 questions and a lot of white space. Hmm, I thought; another slick item in the "one-minute" genre? Another gimmick for raking in big-time royalties? When I observed that this text-sparse paperback was already in its 30th printing and had been translated into 15 languages, my skepticism became laced with several emotions, including envy (why couldn't *I* come up with a clever way to turn a simple idea into a spectacular blockbuster?).

Stock poses questions about values, beliefs, and behaviors—questions that people need to ask themselves and discuss with others, but sometimes are reluctant to raise. These are questions with no right or wrong answers, but questions whose exploration can lead to rewarding discussions and self-growth.

If the *Book* is a gimmick, it's certainly a well-intentioned gimmick. And obviously successful.

I began to realize that perhaps I may have been selling Stock a bit short. I recalled key questions I had devised in the past that had educed productive answers. For example, when working with an advisee who was undecided about courses or major, I often posed this: "If you had complete freedom to do exactly what you want to do in the next 24 hours, without taking into account work, family, or other commitments and responsibilities, what would you do?" The response usually helped the student clarify her/his thinking, leading toward more intelligent decisions.

When investigating a position or program on another campus, I might try to knife through the Everything's Great Façade by asking, "Disregarding the constraints of budget, approval of your boss, and politics, what three changes or innovations would you like to make in the structure or activities of your agency?" I usually got frank answers that were revealing and useful.

Once when anticipating meeting in a reception line a candidate for the presidency of our college, I pondered what question I could ask that could be answered in 60 seconds and still tell me something significant. I came up with this: "During your visit to our campus, what three questions do you most want to ask and have answered?" Values often can be assessed by the questions a person asks.

As teachers, we know the importance of asking questions effectively (whether in class or on tests) and of teaching *students* how to ask their own questions. But all too seldom do we turn important questions on ourselves. I began to speculate on some of the key questions we should be reflecting upon and discussing with our colleagues. Here's my list.

- What activities in teaching give me the greatest satisfaction? What causes me to come away from a class feeling really high?

- What do I do that seems to produce good response in students—not just positive comments but eager attention, intelligent questions, and desire to engage the material?

- What modifications can I make in my teaching in order to increase the frequency of the wonderful moments referred to above?

- Why did I decide to go into teaching? How can I work to enhance the attainment of the goals implied in that choice?

- What values inform my teaching?

- What are my greatest personal strengths and talents? How can I bring these resources to bear more directly and more fully on my teaching?

- What emerging emphases of my department and my college could be aided by the application of my personal strengths and talents?

- In what personal and professional activities would I like to be engaged five years from now? What sequence of steps can I initiate now to bring these goals to fruition?

- If I had the freedom to spend the next day doing exactly what I want (without regard to schedule, commitments, and responsibilities), what would I do?

- If I had the power (without constraints of budget, approval, or politics) to make three changes in my teaching and professional activities, what would they be?

- If I could communicate only five concepts, principles, and values to my students, what would they be?

- If I were to present my very last lecture to students or conduct my last class session, what would it contain?

- If I were to write my own obituary, what would I say (or like to be able to say) about the accomplishments in my life's work?

- Which of my teaching colleagues and administrators do I like to work with the *least*? Why? What steps could *I* initiate to improve our working relationship?

- What three questions about teaching and teachers do *I* think are the most important to ask and have answered?

Of course, this short list of questions for teachers is by no means exhaustive, but it's a good start. I find that dealing with questions usually leads to more questions—questions that are better and more refined. A good question, as John Ciardi put more eloquently, "is not a bolt to be tightened in place, but a seed to be planted and to bear more seed toward the hope of greening the landscape of idea."

This list might be rather overwhelming if considered in its entirety and in depth. But selected questions could be considered in a variety of ways, either individually or in subsets. For example, your department could choose two or three of them (perhaps reframed as appropriate to local circumstances) and program 30-45 minutes into department meetings for consideration of them one at a time. Less formally, the next time you are having lunch with colleagues, you might toss one of the questions into the conversation. Or you could organize an informal interdisciplinary group to consider several over the course of a semester.

On a more personal level, you could select several of the questions, write each with a bold marking pen on a 5x8 card, and post one card per month on the bulletin board or wall over your desk. Think about the question whenever you have a few spare moments. Before you replace a card at the end of the month, take 20 to 30 minutes to write a response on the back of the card.

Engaging in reflective activities such as these is bound to have good effects on our work. It will result in better teaching—and correspondingly better learning by our students. Academic life should be characterized by the continual asking of questions—not just in search of knowledge, but also in search of meaning.

It's easy for us to feel that with all our many responsibilities we don't have time for introspection, not even a few spare minutes here and there. But can any of us who aspire to excellence not afford to take time to reflect deliberately upon our life and our work?

And *that* question is rhetorical.

Response

34

Strategic Teaching: The Possible Dream

By discovering our personal talents, strengths, and resources and applying them toward attainable goals, we can realize our fullest potential and become the teachers we really can be.

> *. . . within the limits set by our innate abilities, we should strive for excellence, for the best that we can do.*
>
> —Hans Selye

One of the most important days of my life was the day that I realized that I would never become a Great Teacher.

That day was a long time a-coming. I remember reading *Goodbye, Mr. Chips* in my youth. It left a lasting impression on me. I resolved to become a beloved teacher like Chips.

By the time I finished high school, tucked into a corner of my cranium was an image of walking down a leaf-strewn campus lane on an early September evening, bathed in the soft light from gas street lamps, on my way to library or seminar, leaving a faint trail of fragrant smoke from a Holmesian pipe.

I went to university and graduate school. I made good grades. I started teaching.

In my late twenties, a visiting professor spent a year on our campus. Woody played the banjo, sang folk songs, and was very popular with students. I saw him as an outstanding teacher, a Great Teacher. He was the embodiment of the charisma I hoped to have.

In my thirties, my Great Teacher image expanded to include a rating of 10 in each category on the form students used to evaluate my teaching. My dream continued. I would be a Star of the highest magnitude, a Triple-Threat Teacher, Super-Prof.

As I neared forty, reality set in. I had yet to find that beautiful autumn scene on a campus. I re-read *Chips* and to my surprise I found it didn't exist there, either. Students' evaluations of my teaching continued to be a mixed bag. I couldn't even master the ukulele, much less the banjo. I met many more Woodies and I found that I didn't match them any better than I did the original model. I had long since discarded my sophomoric pipe and all the smoking paraphernalia that once cluttered my pockets. I had lived half my life and discovered that, alas, I would not, could not be a Chips. My quest for the Golden Apple would be fruitless.

That was The Day. Frustration. Depression. Quiet desperation. (I learned recently that such a malaise is not uncommon in academic midlife. One researcher calls it Professorial Melancholia and is beginning to study it.) I even considered a permanent move into administration.

That day was, as cliché has it, the beginning of the rest of my life. In the next several years, I took a long look at myself, though I realize now that it was not an organized introspection undertaken consciously. I drifted through several new assignments. I did additional graduate work. I explored a few tangents. I became better acquainted with myself.

I had occasion to retake some vocational interest and preference tests. I found that scientific areas, dominant earlier, were now balanced by artistic areas. Here and there, I participated in exercises that revealed my learning, teaching, and achieving styles. I submitted to a well-known personality inventory (the ENFJ name tag from that experience is still tacked to the bulletin board over my desk). I also noted that many of the "stars" of teaching that I knew sometimes flickered; they had weaknesses as well as strengths. I realized that the ways they deployed those strengths were what produced excellence in their work.

During this time, I did some new things and I did some old things differently. I found myself naturally gravitating toward the things I could do well. If I could not adjust my deficiencies, I moved to areas where they played a lesser role in my life.

The end result was of great importance: by no longer dreaming the impossible dream, I found that I was free to move toward accomplishing a possible dream.

The process I went through was really natural growth, prolonged as it was. Reflecting on my meandering journey, I realized that I might have accomplished the same result in much less time had I been more deliberate about it. I tried to extract the essentials from the experience. I began to call the process "Strategic Teaching" because of its similarity to strategic planning, now common in Academe as well as in business.

The Strategic Teaching Process

As I conceive of it, Strategic Teaching is a process that largely builds on strengths. While it doesn't ignore deficiencies, particularly those which can be corrected, it doesn't dwell on weaknesses.

Thus, if a teacher wishes to engage in Strategic Teaching, the first step is assessing personal strengths and resources. While various self-assessment inventories (such as Myers-Briggs Personality Type and Canfield Instructional Styles) may be employed to advantage, they are not essential to the process. Re-reading student evaluations or having a trusted colleague observe and report on teaching can provide abundant useful information.

Additionally, a teacher may simply list strengths or discover them by responding to questions such as:

- What do I enjoy most about teaching?
- In courses or classes that have gone well, with what activities am I especially pleased and satisfied?
- To what activities and teaching behaviors do students seem to have responded well?
- What methods or activities in teaching have I particularly selected over alternatives?
- What beliefs and values relevant to teaching do I hold?

For example, among the strengths I have been able to identify in my own case are these: spontaneity, ability to ask questions that guide student thought and behavior, a knack for designing participative learning exercises, ability to organize class sessions as a series of short scenes in order to maximize student attention. Some of the things I value are cooperation, creativity, freedom, harmony, integrity, responsibility and respect.

A second step, closely related to the first, is delineating the conditions and circumstances that a teacher would like to have characterize teaching. These should always be "possibles"— that is, they should be within personal capabilities already held or attainable through reasonable training or commitment. It may be poetic and noble to seek the impossible dream, but it can be depressing and debilitating to not achieve it.

Again, let me illustrate from personal experience. In my own teaching, I realized that I had been using an instructor-centered approach more than I wanted. I preferred to shift to a student-centered mode, engaging students more actively in the material of mathematics and its applications. This was a condition attainable in part by means of reminding myself to ask questions more frequently (ability to frame questions was a strength I had listed). I could also employ movement more strategically in the course of my presentations—e.g., moving toward students when I wanted to engage them more in dialogue.

In addition, I wanted my class sessions to be more dynamic and less staid. This could be accomplished in part through a heightened mental set that I could achieve by taking a few minutes prior to each class to concentrate on the topic and its mode of presentation. I also wanted to develop more modulation in my voice, which required concentration as well as a little practice—both relatively easy to accomplish. (On the other hand, singing a few appropriate measures, which on rare occasion could contribute to certain presentations I make, strange as that may seem, might well be beyond my capability. Even if I could manage it, considerable training would be required for it to be successful.)

Step three is listing needs and goals, both short-term and long-term, of the department and college. Particular attention should be directed toward how these needs and goals might be changing in response to evolving circumstances in the constituencies served by the college as well as evolving circumstances in society in general. For example, in this phase of Strategic

Teaching a list might include items such as computer literacy, writing across the curriculum, greater involvement of students in the learning process, preparing students for dealing with ethical issues, promoting community involvement and service, vocational preparation, emphasis on independent and lifelong learning, interdisciplinary studies, accommodating and responding to diversity among people, and serving nontraditional students.

Step four is matching, insofar as possible, strengths and resources identified in the first step with items listed in steps two and three. To be sure, it is quite possible and appropriate to capitalize on strengths without their being instrumental to the accomplishment of personal or institutional goals. Yet advancing such goals provides a special incentive to carry out the process and represents Strategic Teaching at perhaps its fullest and finest.

Step five is deciding what actions to take in response to the outcomes of the first four steps and then devising a plan for carrying out those actions. A sensible plan would project activities for both the short-run and the long-run. It would specify in what areas of teaching the activities would occur and when they would occur. The first activity might be one that carries the prospect of highly significant results. Or the plan might begin with a few activities that are relatively easy to carry out, with more to be added as progress is made. The plan of action should be flexible. And it should include an evaluation component, some relatively simple means of assessing the extent to which activities are accomplishing their intended purposes.

Step six is carrying out the plan. Since the plan is flexible, it can accommodate some adjustments in timing that may be dictated by circumstances. Since criteria for success are included, frequent monitoring can lead to modifications even as activities are ongoing.

Perhaps the most important step of all in the process is reflecting on the experience and then responding accordingly. By assessing level of accomplishment, it may be possible to devise ways of refining an activity in order to increase its yield. By examining how an activity has worked in one area, it may be possible to design adaptations to other areas. Carrying out the plan may suggest new options to include in future plans.

Thus, this seventh step is not at all a final step; it only completes one cycle of what may well be a continuous process.

Clarification of the Process

The following example of Strategic Teaching in action may help clarify the concept and the process.

Dr. Ecks, a soft-spoken professor of government, had become increasingly uncomfortable with delivering hour-long, intricately-planned lectures in PS 121, an introductory course crammed with 100 students. One spring, she took time to tally her personal strengths in teaching. Among them she listed "ability to organize activities" (she was somewhat a perfectionist) and "facility in working with students, both in groups and in individual conferences." At the same time, her college was urging faculty members to try to involve students more directly and more actively in the learning process; the college also was searching for ways to include more vocational orientation in its traditional liberal arts program.

During the summer, Dr. Ecks talked with her department chair and negotiated a revision in course procedure. That fall, in PS 121 she gave only two full lectures per week. Every third class she presented a short introductory statement, did a live interview with a local political leader, and conducted a discussion among a panel of a dozen students (she changed the panel members each week). The final five to ten minutes of that hour were devoted to questions from the rest of the students to the panel.

Toward the end of the semester, one of the scheduled guests had a conflict at class time. Instead of a live appearance, the interview was videotaped, and the presentation worked almost as well. Dr. Ecks realized that taping a majority of the interviews was an efficient way to use the new method without imposing on guests by inviting them over and over. She received a grant to do that for the next year.

The revised format worked well and Dr. Ecks continued it. In the third year, she adjusted the pattern so that discussions comprised half the class sessions, alternating with lectures. By that time, she had relocated the course to a room where eight subgroups could discuss the interview simultaneously. The final ten minutes of each discussion class were devoted to brief reports from two or three of the groups. Dr. Ecks also enlisted and trained senior students majoring in government to conduct the discussions; they received one credit in a practicum that helped prepare them for graduate school.

Students nicknamed the course "Grassroots Government," and it became one of the most popular options for satisfying a divisional distribution requirement. A second section was scheduled. Dr. Ecks found her new teaching activity refreshing, and she was very pleased with the results.

This example illustrates several important aspects of Strategic Teaching:

- It need not be a massive, comprehensive makeover, exploiting all a faculty member's strengths toward the accomplishment of many objectives. Initially, it might direct just one or two strengths toward one or two goals. Indeed, the process frequently works better when a faculty member concentrates on one aspect at a time and directs it to a specific course.
- Effectiveness is enhanced when the institution responds and adapts to the strengths of each individual teacher, just as individuals respond and adapt to their own strengths and institutional needs.
- Strategic Teaching is not simply a one-shot affair. It is a continuous process in which revision builds on revision and success breeds success.

In the case of Dr. Ecks, impressive results came about through extended effort. However, the process of Strategic Teaching can be more modest. Consider Prof. Wye, a faculty member who observed colleagues whose classes always seemed to get off to a lively start. He noticed how their opening activities—even the way they entered the room—energized students. He thought to himself, "Hey, I can do some things like that; I've had a little acting experience in college." He discarded his former style of sauntering into the room, casually sitting on the edge of the desk, staring at the clock, and waiting for students to arrive. He developed and used a variety of planned entrances and openings which generated student interest and activity. His approach required relatively little effort, yet produced significant dividends. Caught up with the similarity between theatre and classroom, Prof. Wye eventually drew further upon his stage experience to incorporate other new techniques into his teaching.

The cases of Ecks and Wye differ considerably from typical campus situations. The experience of Dr. Zie, a teacher approaching his tenure decision year, is more common. He and his department chair were in conference, discussing Zie's latest student evaluations of his teaching in Course 104, which included a number of favorable ratings. But there also were comments such as "He speaks softly; it's easy for my mind to wander," "The course isn't very exciting," and "I wonder what use this course is." Most of the conversation between Zie and the chair focused on the negative comments. He protested that his voice was naturally soft, and he didn't know what to do about it. She suggested that he might consider taking voice lessons. He asked about ways to make the course more interesting and practical. She couldn't seem to suggest anything other than "work harder at it." (Her response was very much like teachers' common admonishment to low-achieving students: "Study harder.") The two of them, both well-meaning individuals, largely ignored the positive comments on the evaluations as well as Zie's strengths. The conference became a frustrating half-hour for both parties. When he left, Dr. Zie was depressed and worried about his future at the college. (If this portrayal sounds familiar, it may be because many teachers find themselves in similar circumstances—or because we have within our acquaintance a Dr. Zie who gets little help in becoming a better teacher.)

Even if Dr. Zie were to discover some ways to improve in his areas of weakness, most of his efforts would likely be reactive, focussed on a few negative comments in a specific course. Typically, he might give little attention and time to capitalizing on his strengths. In contrast, the process of Strategic Teaching is largely *proactive*, accenting and enhancing positive qualities. There is a world of difference between these two approaches.

Among the benefits to faculty who engage in Strategic Teaching are increased comfort and satisfaction from teaching—and perhaps even joy from the endeavor. Strategic Teaching helps keep academic work vital, exciting, and refreshing. It can help combat Professorial Melancholia, post-tenure slump, the dead-wood syndrome, and other maladies (real or imagined) to which faculty members are said to be susceptible.

Of course, the greatest beneficiaries of Strategic Teaching are students. Better teaching will likely result in increased learning. Further, a teacher who is visibly striving to use personal resources to the fullest is clearly a good role model for students.

Strategic Teaching is a means of using human resources sensibly, effectively, and efficiently. It could become an important dimension in fulfilling higher education's mission in the predicted forthcoming era of reduced pools of professional teaching talent. Especially in that era, all teachers will need to distribute their efforts wisely.

Making the Process Work

The Strategic Teaching concept may seem rather straightforward and uncomplicated. It's meant to be. But even simple concepts require care, diligence, and often dedication to put them into operation successfully.

For one thing, a process of building on strengths often seems a bit unnatural for many teachers. Oddly enough, we seem to have a natural tendency to focus, sometimes excessively, on weaknesses and their correction. Engaging in Strategic Teaching requires a change in behavior quite like successful weight control. In weight control, reducing caloric intake is important, but long-term results occur only with commitment to a different style of eating and living. Strategic Teaching may well require teachers to look at themselves and their roles from a new perspective.

By saying that Strategic Teaching involves concentrating on strengths and using them to enhance effectiveness of performance, I'm not suggesting that weaknesses be ignored. Overcoming correctable weaknesses does warrant attention as long as the primary focus on strengths is not sacrificed.

Strategic Teaching must be a genuine personal endeavor, motivated by a desire to come as close as possible to the teacher our innate abilities allow us to be. It cannot be something forced on us by others. It requires our acceptance and commitment and, in large part, our personal control.

Moving carefully through the initial phases of Strategic Teaching is appropriate. Obviously, it's inadvisable to develop a strategy for deploying strengths toward the achievement of goals without first determining in considerable detail just what those strengths and goals are. Jumping into an action plan without taking the necessary preparatory steps may risk overlooking significant options.

In selecting goals, aim high—but not too high, of course. Hans Selye, a noted authority on management of stress, cautions that *perfection* is nearly always unattainable. He advises that by not undertaking tasks that are beyond us we can avoid the frustration and humiliation of failure. "Everyone has his own limits. For some of us, these may be near the maximum, for others near the minimum of what man can attain... Excellence is a wonderful goal in itself and highly suitable to earn us the good will, respect, and even love of our neighbors" (Selye, 1974, *Stress without Distress*, Philadelphia, Lippincott, p. 11).

Another criterion for success in Strategic Teaching is detailing the proposed activity and its time schedule in writing. A "plan in mind" often turns out to be no plan at all. A plan doesn't have to be the ultimate in completeness, and it certainly shouldn't be cast in concrete. But it does require the crystallization, clarification, and precision that comes from writing it down.

If you are devising a plan, clearly identify activities and allow enough time to accomplish them. Be sure to include a means for assessing effectiveness. Strategic Teaching is characterized by continual forward movement. An activity is carried out and evaluated; then, revised activity is designed and carried out. As one set of behaviors is learned and consolidated, another set is initiated. A thorough plan might project activities through several such cycles. Be careful to not undertake too much at one time. But also be careful to not undertake less than might be appropriate at a given stage.

Commitment to new behaviors such as Strategic Teaching often involves taking some risks. Though we may try to keep those risks reasonable and sensible, we may not always attain the success that we wish, especially on early trials. Most of us in Academe are uneasy with receiving marks of less than "A" for our own work, but there are valuable lessons to be learned when we fall short of our goals. Benefiting from those lessons by recharting future activity more carefully and effectively can turn even the occasional partial failure into a success. After all, "failure" is really *opportunity*—opportunity to begin again, wiser than before. It's how we reframe our errors that makes the difference. We may take comfort and inspiration from John Dewey: "Not perfection as a final goal, but the ever-enduring process of perfecting, maturing, refining is the aim of living."

By emphasizing that Strategic Teaching is largely an individual process, I don't mean to imply that it's necessarily a solitary activity. The endeavor can be facilitated through interaction with others. A member of a counseling and testing staff might offer various instruments useful in self-assessment. A trusted colleague or a teaching consultant might provide helpful response to plans and activities. Two faculty members might well work together as each goes through the Strategic Teaching process; verbal commitment to another person gives impetus to carrying out plans and meeting target dates. Of course, the critical element in any collaborative activity always is mutual trust.

The process of Strategic Teaching could be adapted on a departmental or college level in order to deploy the unit's teaching resources effectively. In any such collective activity, it is essential that individual participation remain voluntary. Further, use of the process in a summative way is likely to be counterproductive. Strategic Teaching cannot be a college-wide crusade in which all faculty members are pressured to enlist.

At whatever level Strategic Teaching operates, its overall value will probably be a function of the institution's recognition and commitment to development of individual human resources. If an institution expects all teachers to fit a common mold, if those who don't fit that mold are discarded, then outcomes for faculty who engage in the Strategic Teaching process likely will be diminished. But if an institution values individual worth and fulfillment of human potential, then Strategic Teaching can be a valuable force in achieving excellence.

My own journey toward better teaching has been an adventurous and productive odyssey. Once I became committed to the concept of Strategic Teaching, I found that continuous, gradual, incremental, planned improvement that builds on personal strengths and resources became a way of life. My journey, though slow and undirected at the beginning, has turned into an odyssey without end.

I commend Strategic Teaching as a deliberate process to all teachers who seek to become the best teachers they can be. Few of us may become as beloved as Chips. Few of us may become Great Teachers. But many of us, by dreaming a possible dream, can reach our own excellence. That dream provides us great motivation and its attainment provides us more than sufficient reward.

┌─ Response ──┐
│   │
│   │
│   │
│   │
│   │
│   │
│   │
│   │
│   │
│   │
│   │
│   │
│   │
│   │
└──┘

35

Power in College Teaching

Power appears in many guises. It ebbs and flows, seen or unseen, beneath most teacher-student relationships. It may serve teaching purposes well, but it also may erode the best intentioned efforts.

Power in college teaching is a topic that has drawn the attention of faculty members for many years. We long to use it properly and effectively, and we worry about succumbing to its misuse and abuse.

In conversations with colleagues about this subject, I find that we commonly think about power in two of its more obvious senses. The first of these is maintaining control in the classroom—that is, being able to run through our agenda or accomplish our goals without distraction or disruption, maintaining the authority that derives from our knowledge and position.

The second sense in which we commonly think about power is avoiding the abuses of power. Generally, this involves a compendium of commandments, often unwritten, yet in large part understood and accepted. Among such dicta are: Thou shalt not be arbitrary. Thou shalt not ridicule or hassle students. Thou shalt not use students for thy personal gain. Thou shalt not do power trips.

I don't mean to downplay such injunctions. Of course it's important to treat students with dignity and respect. We all discourage abuse, and we condemn violations, whether major or minor.

And of course it's important to stay on educational track and to maintain reasonable classroom decorum. It's part of our implied contract with students to use class time wisely for learning purposes.

But over the years, I've found that the issue of power in teaching is much more complex than this. Power is an undercurrent that ebbs and flows beneath most of our activities and relationships with students. It may support and reinforce our teaching purposes, but it also may erode some of our best intentioned efforts. It may surface quickly and unexpectedly. And it may lurk in hidden pools and quagmires, waiting for the unwary to misstep.

Power appears in many guises. And it's unseen or unrecognized power that may be the most troublesome for teachers.

Power is often perceived differently by teachers and students.

There is no question that power is available to teachers. We are endowed with power by our disciplines and by the structure of our institutions. Yet, many teachers choose not to overtly exercise this power, preferring to accomplish their missions through less obvious means of encouragement, motivation, example, reason, and persuasion. For many, having to resort to power—for example, using the threat of a grade to obtain compliance with requests or speaking sharply to quiet a disturbing student—represents a breakdown of other strategies. Those of us who are of this mind continually explore alternatives and ask ourselves if we have exhausted all reasonable options before we succumb to employing raw power to achieve our purposes in the classroom.

In reality, we may not have as much choice as we think. Many students in our classes, whether by virtue of their previous educational conditioning or their concept of the roles of student and teacher, perceive us as powerful. If students endow us with power, we *are* powerful, and that will be reflected in their relationships with us, no matter what attempts we may make to lower our power profiles.

Here's an example of such a situation. A student is conferring with me about a subject for a term paper. I try to be helpful and suggest several alternatives in the interest of narrowing the topic to a manageable size. But he takes each suggestion in turn as a mandate, and finally he presses me to identify the best one. I reply that it's his choice. He leaves my office confused and upset because I didn't tell him what to write about.

So, when students grant us more power than we choose to exercise, problems can develop. There is another side to the issue: some students may grant us less power than we may need to exercise in order to fulfill our teaching responsibilities. These students may resist meeting the requirements of a course or may meet them grudgingly or barely within the letter of the syllabus. They may even try to defeat the objectives of the course through less than honorable means.

Of course, we are likely to have both kinds of students in any given course, with many shadings between the extremes. Furthermore, students' perceptions are likely to be in a continual state of flux. And we teachers may vary our exercise of power according to the subject matter, as well as to where we are in a course. Whenever there is a disparity between students' perceptions of a teacher's power and the teacher's own perception and employment of power, tension will result—often to the detriment of accomplishing learning goals. With such a fluid situation, it's no wonder that it's easy for us to become enveloped by the flash floods and quicksands of power.

In almost every situation in which power surfaces, decisions are judgment calls. There seem to be no uniform rules that can be applied with high assurance of success. In my own teaching, I try to cope by seeking answers to some key questions:

- How can I make abundantly clear to my students my goals and expectations?
- How can I assess students' perceptions of my power?
- Can I (and should I) adjust to the disparity in power perceptions?
- How can I affect my students' perceptions of my power in order to bring them closer to the level that I feel is appropriate for me to exercise?
- What level of power *is* appropriate for me to exercise?

Power is inherent in promoting change and learning.

Education is a process of change in students—change in knowledge, change in skills, change in behavior, often even change in attitudes and values. Teachers are agents of that change. With but few exceptions, we impinge on students—sometimes subtly, sometimes intensely. We challenge students. To some of them, however, the process can be discomforting, and they may perceive it as threatening to their well-being and perhaps even a downright violation of their person. Yet, the process of education almost always involves a teacher's exercising power and influence over a student in some way.

Suppose that I try to engage students actively in the learning process by setting up a simulation in which they play assigned roles. Some are developers, some are financiers, some are politicians, and some are concerned citizens; together they are to hammer out a community's policy on growth. It might work well as an educational exercise. Or it might struggle because some students may refuse to play roles that they feel are in violation of their personal principles. Some may react against having to reveal their emotions and values. And some may protest that they are in class to learn from the teacher and pass tests, not to play mickey mouse games.

Or suppose I try to get students to prepare for ethical decisions they'll face in their chosen careers. Since ethical decisions derive from personal values, I devise classroom activities designed to get students to recognize and understand their personal values—and perhaps even to modify them, if they choose. But two weeks later, a delegation of my students calls on the dean to protest that I'm meddling with their personal lives instead of teaching them the subject matter; they say they would have dropped the course if they had known in time that it was going to be like this. I point out to the dean that I've been very careful to disclose up-front what I expect from students, but I'm not sure my arguments convince her.

In both cases, I've directed my power as a teacher legitimately (I think) toward educational goals, but some students think I'm using power improperly. If I try to engage students in stimulating dialogue, some of them may feel inappropriately imposed upon. Some may defer, accepting my arguments as gospel and declining to uphold their own beliefs. Those at relativist stages of development will react differently from the dualists (to use Perry's schema for levels of development in the college years)—and differently yet from the few who may be at a commitment stage. Even in everyday discussion, women tend to respond differently from men.

When I choose to assume a particular position for purposes of discussion, I'm never sure that all my students understand that I'm playing a role (despite the bright red devil's advocate T-shirt I sometimes wear to signal my temporary change in character). And I've found that using satire runs a great risk of total misinterpretation.

Indeed, teaching is an intrusive activity. It's easy for aggressive educational postures to cross over into an adversarial relationship. It's easy for exercise of influence to be interpreted as manipulation. It's easy for requests, challenges, and demands to intrude too far on the persons of students. Even a modest display of power can lead to procedural dilemmas, not to mention the possibility of ethical transgressions.

But unless we are content to be bloodless pedagogues, carrying the title of Teacher in name only, we will have to take some risks. Taking risks knowingly does not mean that we should take them recklessly, however. We must constantly monitor our teaching activity. For myself, I do that by asking more questions:

- How can I be more aware of students' reactions and perceptions?

- Am I dealing with students as individuals insofar as possible?

- Am I treating students autonomously, allowing them the freedom to make their own decisions?

- In challenging situations, do I leave students a sufficient out without providing a too easy cop-out?

- Have my disclosures of the course content and processes been thorough enough to give students every chance of avoiding situations that really might violate their principles?

- Have I shared and discussed with students my concept of my role as teacher, as well as my philosophy of learning and view of power?

Teachers can be models of how to manage power wisely.

Aside from the significant impact on the formal education of students, there is another important aspect involved in how teachers manage the power relationship: the model of power and its exercise that we portray. If we wish our students to become persons who use power wisely in their lives, let them see that quality in us.

Perhaps it's how teachers conceive of power that makes the ultimate difference. Consider this statement by Peter G. Beidler, Professor of English at Lehigh University and CASE Professor-of-the-Year in 1983, in an essay "Why I Teach" (*Alumni Magazine Consortion*, November 1984):

> *And I have power. I have the power to nudge, to fan sparks, to ask troubling questions, to praise an attempted answer, to condemn hiding from the truth, to suggest books, to point out a pathway. What other power matters?*

Many of us share this viewpoint. That positive and wise use of power to advance learning, to change lives for the better, to affect eternity through our students is what makes teaching such a noble—and yes, *powerful* enterprise.

Response

Afterword: A Few Notes and Reflections on Writing

At a conference a few years ago, I attended a session on how to write an article for a professional journal. The presenter went through all the conventional steps of targeting an audience and a journal, researching material, recording it on cards, arranging the cards logically, writing topical sentences, writing paragraphs, revising them, and framing a conclusion. And then, when everything else is done, she said, go back and read the article carefully and choose a title that fits it.

I was struck with the contrast of that process with how I usually write an article: Some event or activity causes an idea to pop into my head. The setting I'm in may trigger a thought. (At the moment of this writing, I'm looking out a window at a thunderstorm rolling down from Mt. Evans, wondering if this inspiring scene will prompt something in the writing portion of my brain.) I mull the idea or thought around in my head for a while, maybe even days or weeks. I search for meaning. I ponder on it. I try to find a title that encompasses what I've been thinking about, since a good title sharpens the focus of writing. When that title finally jells, I know that I'm almost ready to sit down and do some serious writing. But first I fine-tune the title into a form that's apt to grab readers—for example: "Coaching Mathematics and Other Academic Sports." (When people hear that title, invariably they chuckle or smile broadly; it seems to strike their imagination.)

My next step likely is to consider a possible ending, some sort of twist or flair that will send readers away still actively engaged in the subject and, I hope, contemplating what to do about it. The ending eventually gets some fine-tuning, too, but that can come later.

Then I back up to the beginning. I think about how to get into the subject in a way that will continue to draw the attention that was captured by the title. Incorporating visual characteristics in the opening sentences (as well as later) helps to do that. For example,"It was one of those gorgeous autumn afternoons: a deep October blue sky contrasted with the brilliant crimsons and golds of the trees, the dazzle of the sun moderated the crispness in the air, and the spirit of the homecoming crowd brought the stadium to vibrant life. It was a perfect day for football."

I work over a means to take me from my beginning to my ending in the most direct way. Often it's a modified narrative of whatever experience triggered my thoughts in the first place. Sometimes it's building upon the metaphor that informs the article or trying to make connections between two seemingly unrelated things. Or I may get started on an off-beat idea and continue to plumb the possibilities of that perspective. Occasionally imagination runs wild to concoct a fantasy piece (the muse must have quaffed a few double-meads before tapping me on the shoulder). In any case, once the direction is cast the text often rolls naturally. If I'm lucky.

If I'm not lucky, I agonize over my inability to work things out. I worry that I don't really have a handle on the subject. Sometimes I put what I've written aside and wait for something to bring it back to the front burner. If inspiration doesn't strike, the piece sits in limbo. I hate to admit how many half-finished (a few perhaps half-baked) articles are piled on my back burner at this moment. But it's better to have gotten something on paper or in computer even if the piece is not fleshed out. At some point the Zeigarnik effect, the compulsion for closure, may take hold and the article gets finished.

In pre-computer days when I started with pencil drafts, I'd scratch up the first sheets until I could barely follow my scribbles. Then I'd type a rough draft and scratch it up some more. The next typed draft often was good enough to send out to several friends who function as my personal reviewers. Their comments and suggestions would be incorporated into a third draft, which perhaps needed only a little cutting and pasting before being shipped off to an editor. This labor-intensive process is compressed considerably now in this age of word processors. But the point still can be made that the essence of writing is extensive revision, even up to the final reading of proof sheets from the printer. And some pieces are never really completely finished—only abandoned.

There are notable exceptions to the writing process I describe. "Coaching Mathematics and Other Academic Sports," the seminal and arguably most successful article I've written, was dashed off in a single sitting of 45 minutes at a conference at Chateau Montebello in Quebec. I spent another 45 minutes preparing a clean draft using a typewriter at the registration desk, revising as I typed. The piece was accepted within two days, and I spent a couple of hours fine-tuning it following the conference. Subsequent to publication, it has been reprinted over twenty times, and it gained me a reputation as a "math coach," as well as a brief interview in *The Chronicle of Higher Education*. It's been used in many settings. Each time Bill Pfeifle programs it into a seminar, he pays me a compliment that I prize highly: "I wouldn't change a single word of it!" he says. Neither would I (but for this book I did adjust a couple of commas in the piece). I've never been able to replicate that rapid process with another article, nor have I been able to produce a piece that I think has been written as well or has been as widely recognized.

Another exception often occurs when I'm invited to write on a specific subject or when I spontaneously and arbitrarily assign myself a topic. For one thing, these pieces are usually more sober than what I customarily write. They're on the edge of my element. And I struggle with them.

"Power in College Teaching" is a case in point. I played with seven or eight approaches and configurations for over six months before I found one that I considered satisfactory. And I knew I was in trouble when I couldn't settle on a title before (and even during) writing. I finally copped out with a mundane title supported with an extended opening blurb, and I reluctantly released the piece to the editor of *Teaching Excellence* barely within deadline. Even though it has been well-received and even though I use it in workshops, I still didn't attain what I wanted before having to abandon it.

My strategy for coping with situations like this is to try to avoid them if I can. Playing to one's strengths is a sound rule of thumb in writing—or in anything. (At the same time, I recognize that good results and learning often follow from accepting new challenges in areas where one initially may feel uncomfortable or lacking in skill.)

Experts recommend setting aside a regular time and special place for writing. It's good advice. I'm seldom able to follow it myself, due to other commitments that sometimes take priority at that regular time and special place. But I keep trying. Most of the time these days, the special place is in front of a computer, often after midnight. If I need particular inspiration in getting started, I may retreat to the patio, bask in fresh air and the sights and sounds of nature, take in hand that old-fashioned implement called a pencil, and try to call the spirits to inspire me. (If that doesn't produce results, at least I've been able to enjoy a pleasant interlude.) That strategy doesn't work very well in cool weather, of course, though I've been known to build a little fire in a pit at the edge of the patio and create what I call a cabin simulation while I ponder what to write. I like to have hard copy with me to work on when time becomes available unexpectedly in airports and on planes. There's something about winging through the atmosphere at 32,000 feet, sans telephone and other interruptions, that helps the creative juices flow.

I find that I often get good ideas in the shower, and I sometimes outline an entire project or article in my head. Albert Einstein once advised, "Make friends with your shower. If inspired to sing, maybe the song has an idea in it for you." But those ideas must be written down immediately upon exiting the shower; I've lost a number of good ones by waiting to get dried and dressed and to my desk to make notes. And there have been many times just before falling asleep at night when I thought I had a great idea that I couldn't possibly forget by morning—but on awakening I found it had escaped. Inspiration may suddenly strike at any moment and it can depart just as suddenly; it's a good idea to have pencil and paper always handy to capture it before it evaporates.

Sometimes the opposite happens. An idea finds its way into my head and begins rattling around. I think of its ramifications. I relate it to other ideas. Soon my brain becomes cluttered with all this, and I can't think of anything else. I'm distracted; my to-do list for the day or week begins to collect dust. The only solution is to get the thoughts out of my head and onto paper. The result may or may not be a usable piece, but no matter— my brain is clear again for other things. James Still, a venerable Kentucky writer, has told me he experiences a similar phenomenon from time to time. Zora Neale Hurston put it well: "There is no agony like bearing an untold story inside you."

Let me return to my opening paragraph. I want to be careful to not do injustice to the presenter I spoke of therein. Her approach to writing is just as valid for her as mine is for me.

And hers is more valid for research reports and the like, which is what she was focused on. My approach may be better for freer flowing pieces that often spring out of one's head. I make the comparison to emphasize that styles vary widely. Lucky are the persons who discover what method works best for them and then exploit it. In my case, it took a long time to arrive at that point. Chalk it up to slow learning. Or perhaps lack of attention to the lessons to be discovered about writing. No matter; I finally found my style.

And that is to say that I finally found my voice, however strange a voice it might be. I realized that I might have something to say. I figured out how to say it—succinctly and from a novel perspective. I found that my genre was short pieces, rather than long ones. And I discovered that enough people both wanted to hear what I had to say and found it useful. Who could ask for anything more? (Well, I wish I had learned these things sooner...)

Bob Boice once told me that a writer does not have to be one-hundred percent original in order to produce worthwhile articles. There is a place for the unusual perspective, the new configuration, the different way of saying things—somewhat like old wine in new skins. I finally took him seriously. And William Zinsser advises always writing to please oneself first; if the writing also pleases others, so much the better.

There are many writing voices and there are many writing styles. Voice and style must be discovered for one's self.

So why have I gone on at such length about my writing? I think I've done so in order to encourage readers to examine their own writing and to get better in tune with their own voices and styles. I want them to consider writing more in order to share their ideas with others and to gain the benefits of clarifying their own thinking through writing. I guess I'm just expressing in another way and reinforcing some of the things that Boice, Zinsser, and many others have said.

But as much as anything, I'm communicating that writing can bring enjoyment, satisfaction, and affirmation. It's opportunity to share and to influence. It may not always be easy, but it's rewarding in many ways.

That's why I do it. I hope that's why you will do it. More power to you!

By Way of Acknowledgment

Most books are not the result of effort by a single person, and this one is no exception. Many persons helped make these writings possible and deserve credit (but I hope not blame) for this collection of short pieces. Let me now recognize a few of them.

The first of these is Steve Scholl, whose encouragement—indeed, insistence—at the 1982 conference of the Professional and Organizational Development Network in Higher Education led to the writing of an article on coaching mathematics. Steve is followed immediately by LuAnn Wilkerson, whose strong support was instrumental in pushing the piece through an editorial committee reluctant to accept a somewhat unconventional article.

That article appeared in POD's book of resource readings a year later. Joyce Povlacs Lunde asked to reprint it in the University of Nebraska's newsletter, and there followed a wave of additional requests for reprints that by now has exceeded twenty. Those many editors whose names are buried somewhere in my files stimulated me to write several other short, off-beat pieces. These, too, met with favorable response, and the writing continued—clear testimony of the fruits of reinforcement.

My younger and more irreverant son Karl often warned people of what he considered the dangers of this reinforcement: "Don't encourage him!" he urged. But that seemed to be of no avail, and the consequence for their ignoring his advice was more articles and more reprints.

Somewhere amidst this binge of writing, I wrote a strange piece on football being played by math students. An editor agreed to print it but later suffered a change of mind. Jim Eison, then editor of *The Journal of Staff, Program, & Organization Development*, heard of this and snapped up the piece, suggesting that it be the first in a regular series of similar articles—thus giving birth to the Chalk Dust columns.

Jim deserves additional mention in this listing of acknowledgments. He pays me one of the finest compliments I could receive on my work: "He always makes me think." Jim granted me a freedom that few writers enjoy, and that kept the creative juices flowing. I thank Karron Lewis, Jim's successor as editor, for continuing that policy. And while speaking of the *Journal*, I must include publishers Doug and Gayla Dollar who provide both great support and great cooperation.

Bill McKeachie sends me nice notes when he sees one of my articles, and he often distributes copies to his graduate students. Ohmer Milton has fed me abundant material over the years. Betty Spohn reprinted a number of pieces in her *TIPS Newsletter*. Al Menlo was one of the first to suggest that the pieces be collected and made available as triggers for discussions in courses on teaching and in seminars and luncheons for faculty members. Maryellen Weimer has greatly extended my readership through reprinting some of my pieces in *The Teaching Professor*, which she edits.

The list of reinforcers could go on and on. I thank the many readers of Chalk Dust who have taken time to convey kind comments and support.

There is one other, small circle that merits special mention. No draft of an article, whether rough or smooth, passes from my hands without a reading by Donna Fisch, my wife; her simple but positive "Yeah" is required confirmation that the subject is worth pursuing further. Among those whose editorial advice I seek on occasion are LeAne Rutherford and Ken Zahorski.

I save the most important credit for last. At the front of this book, there is a cryptic dedication to "E.E.W." Those initials stand for Elsie Weekly. Our friendship stretches back to Hiram College days, when she was dean of students and I was associate dean. Our collaboration on many things began then and has continued through these many years. (I especially remember my having to translate for her the four-letter words that students painted on the watertower; she in turn taught me how to speak Hoosier.) Most of the articles in this collection have had the benefit of her careful attention and critical, yet friendly editorial advice. I know my writing is much better due to Elsie's review, and I'm grateful for her help.

At the risk of being anticlimactic, I add two more thoughts. In true Chalk Dust fashion, I'd like to make a point out of these acknowledgments. The persons listed above (and many others) have provided affirmation of my work and my person. That affirmation provides more than just reinforcement to continue.

It provides great satisfaction. It provides true intrinsic reward. It provides the well-being which Hans Selye says is necessary to deal with the challenges and stresses of life so that they do not become distresses. It's something that I've found without really seeking it. I feel that I have been truly blessed in this regard. And my hope is that you, too, may be so blessed in your life and your work.

Finally, I remind you of my son's caveat. Heed his warning, unless you are willing to be subjected to a second round of crazy pieces. What would it be called? *Return of the Chalk Dust Collection? Chalk Dust Strikes Again? Still More Chalk Dust Yet Already? Chalk Dust—The Next Generation?* As my father (who had seeds of a writer in him) often said: It staggers the imagination!